AF263522

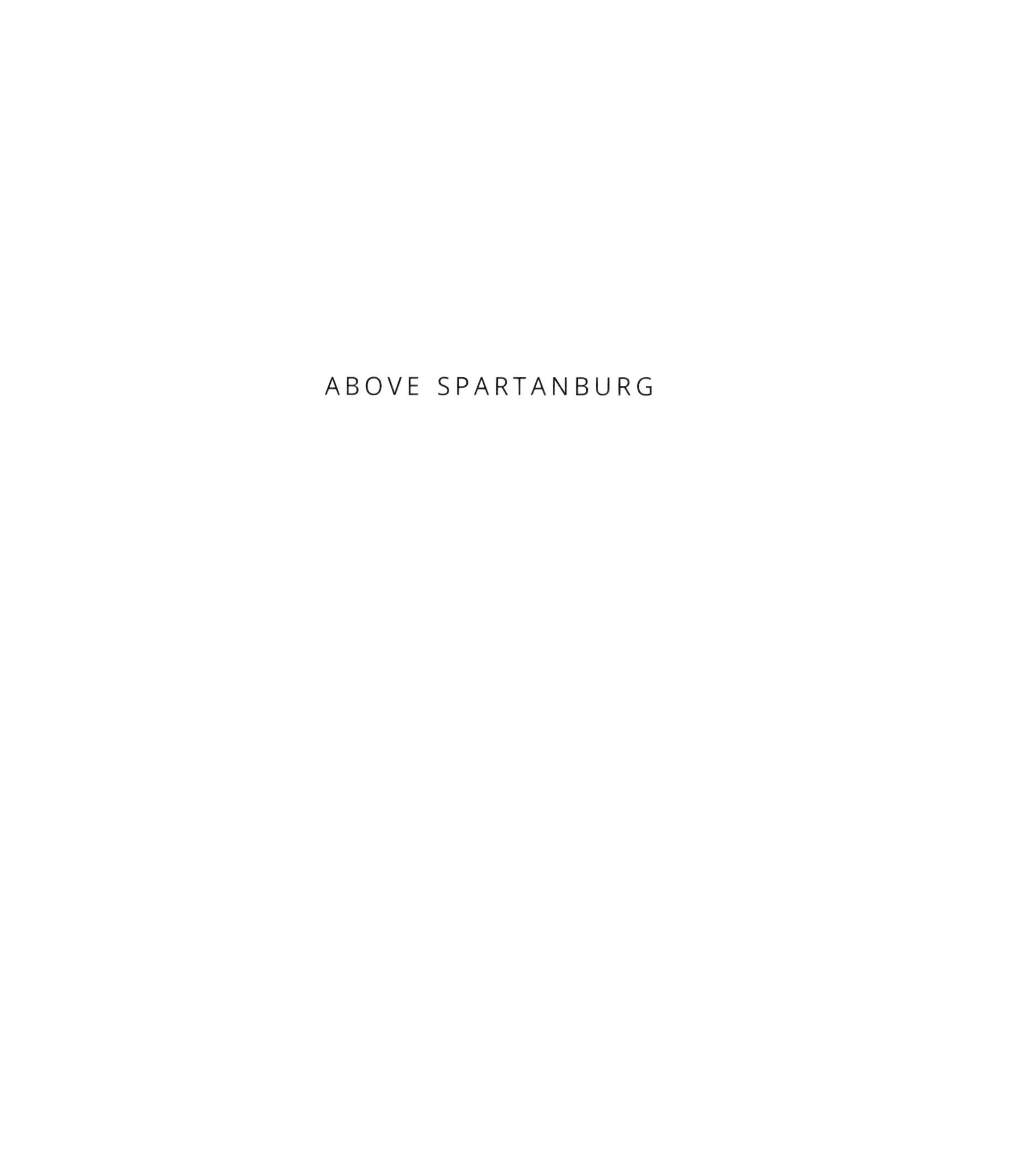

ABOVE SPARTANBURG

ABOVE SPARTANBURG

IMAGES by KAVIN BRADNER

HUB CITY WRITERS PROJECT
SPARTANBURG, SC

Photography: Kavin Bradner / @abovespartanburg
Book Design: Kate McMullen
Cover Design: Meg Reid
Editing and Proofreading: Betsy Teter

Printed in East Peoria, IL by Versa Press

Library of Congress Cataloging-in-Publication Data Applied for
www.loc.gov

ISBN: 978-1-938235-68-9 paperback

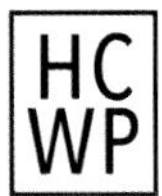

Hub City Writers Project
186 West Main St.
Spartanburg, SC 29306
1.864.577.9349
www.hubcity.org | @hubcitywriters

Images for me are more than just something pretty to look at: they're a way of life. They help me preserve time spent with friends and family, the adventures had, and the ones still to come. Above Spartanburg was born out of adventures with close friends into abandoned buildings in Spartanburg. I wondered what some of these places, many with caved-in roofs, might look like from the top-down perspective. I thought they were incredible!

I changed the name of an old Instagram account to Above Spartanburg and started sharing images I had taken. But it was winter and not much looked very interesting, so I stopped. In the spring of 2019 I started shooting and posting on the account again. The first image back was a shot looking down at the Masonic Temple. The image went Spartanburg viral-ish, gaining me quite a few followers. People started wondering what was coming next. I realized people were interested in seeing views we all see hundreds of times in our day-to-day lives from an entirely new perspective.

I want to photograph these places in their best light. For me, that is typically just after sunrise or during sunset. I'm not a cinematographer but I like to think I have a film/movie mindset when shooting—from the shadows stretching across some of the images to add depth and feeling to the smooth, beautiful, golden sun lighting the ground. I spend countless hours sitting behind my computer looking for locations on Google Maps, trying to guess how the light will hit the tops of these places and when the best time to go out and photograph them will be.

With each post came new followers and more and more excitement. I didn't have a goal in the beginning. I just started doing it, and only then realized I was doing it because there wasn't anything else like it. I think that's why the account has done so well. I want my images

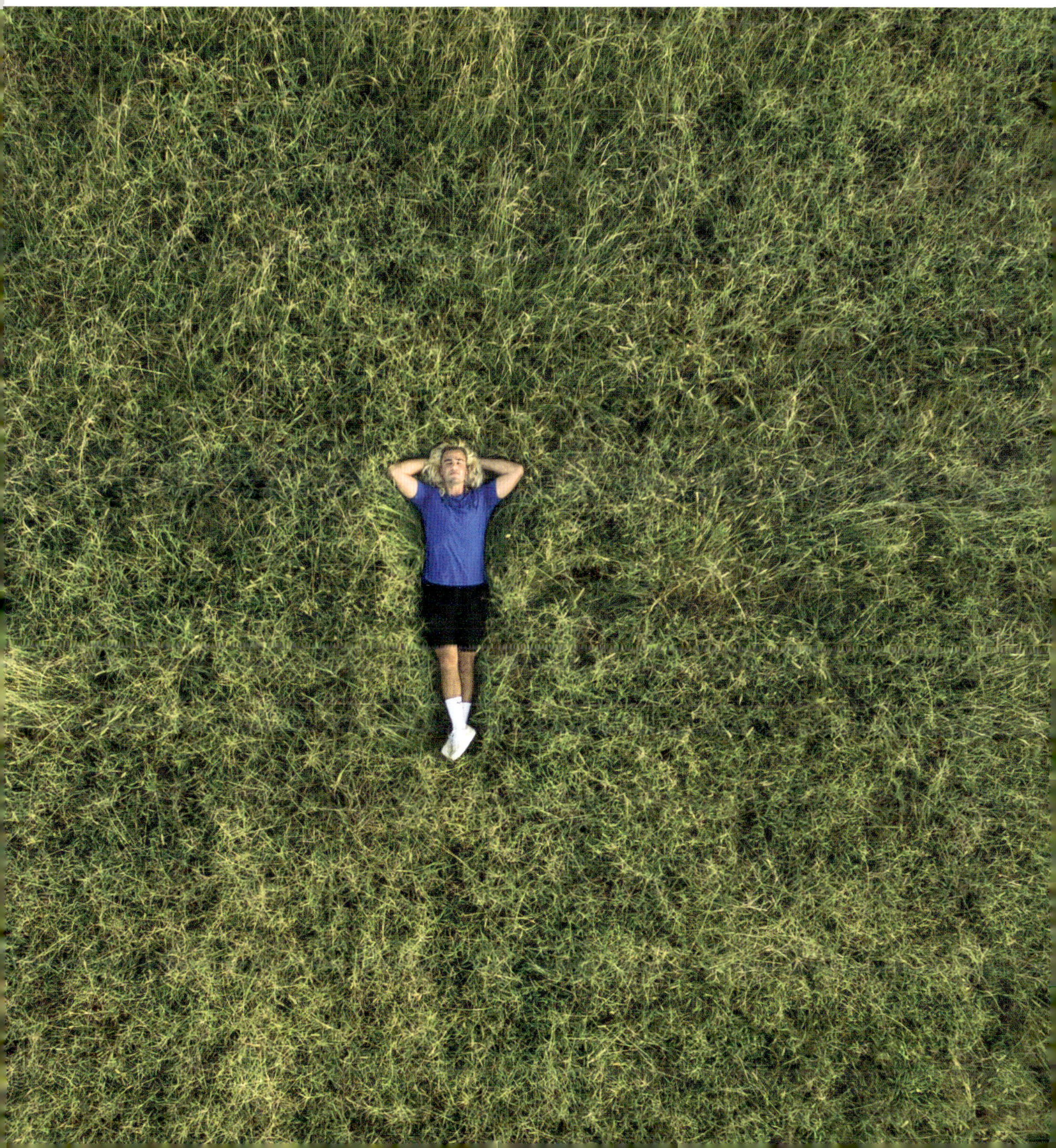

to evoke a sense of new-ness within what is old. I love the feeling of making something look completely different from what it actually is. I want people to be able to look back on my photographs years from now and be glad I shot those places before they were either renovated, torn down, or painted over. I'm so glad the photographers shot our city throughout its many changes, and that their stunning photographs still line the hallways of our downtown library. I hope my images, like theirs, will stick around for generations to come.

—KAVIN BRADNER
NOVEMBER 2019
@abovespartanburg / @bradnerkavin518

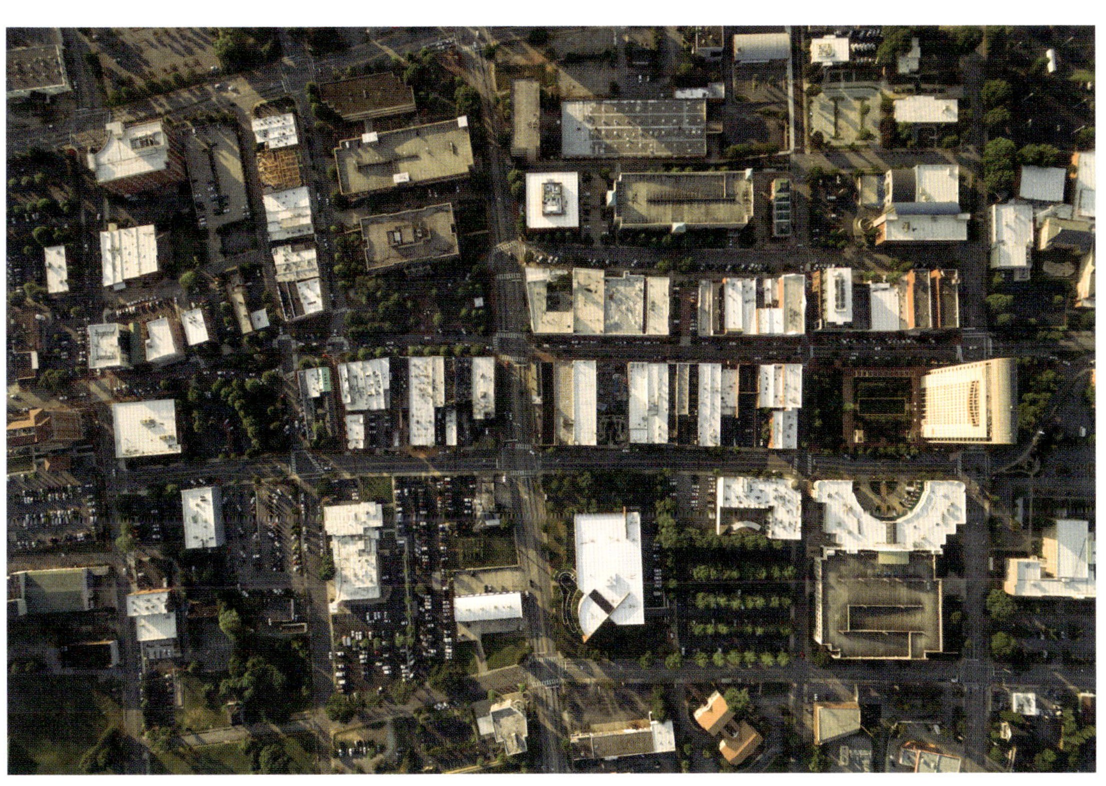

ABOVE DOWNTOWN SPARTANBURG

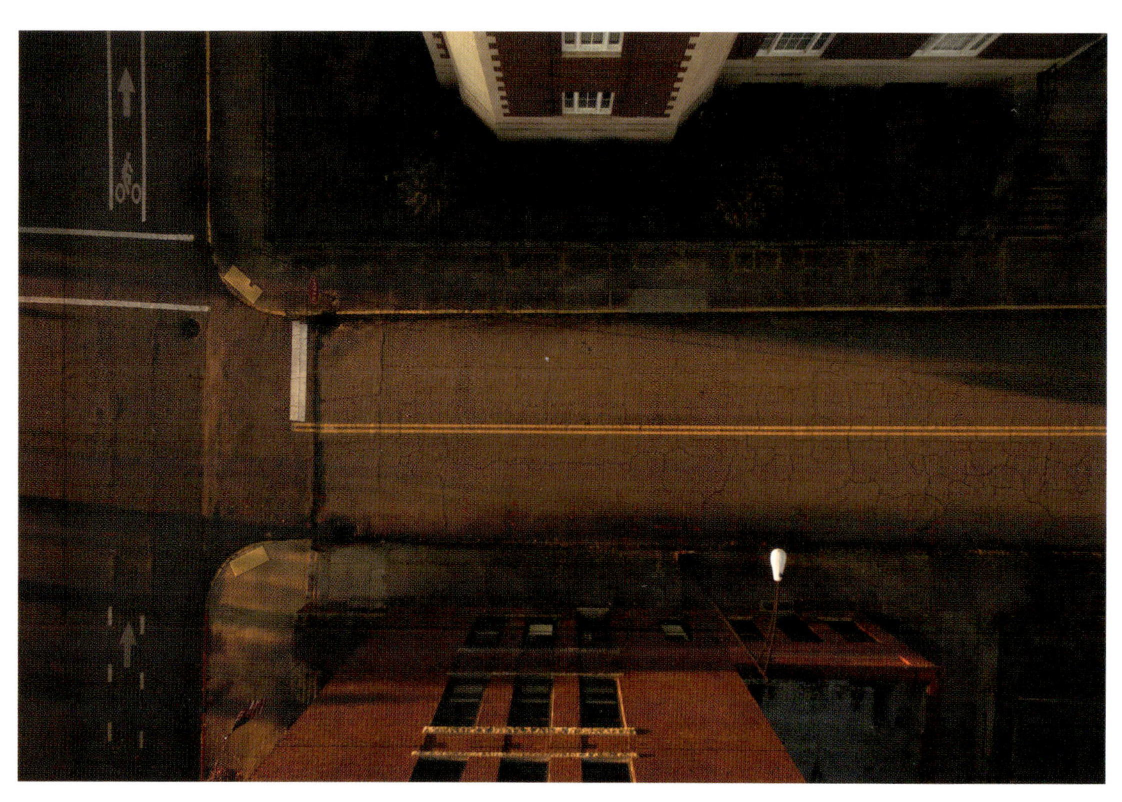

DONALD S. RUSSELL STREET

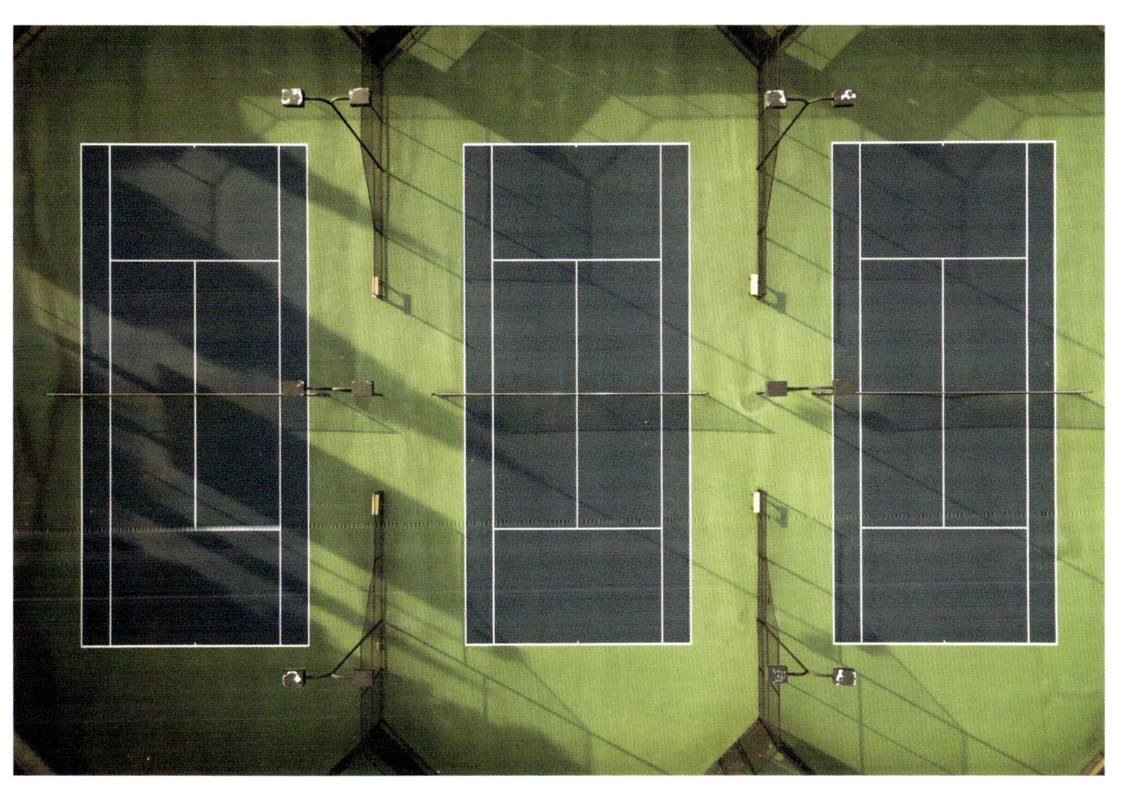

WOFFORD TENNIS COURTS

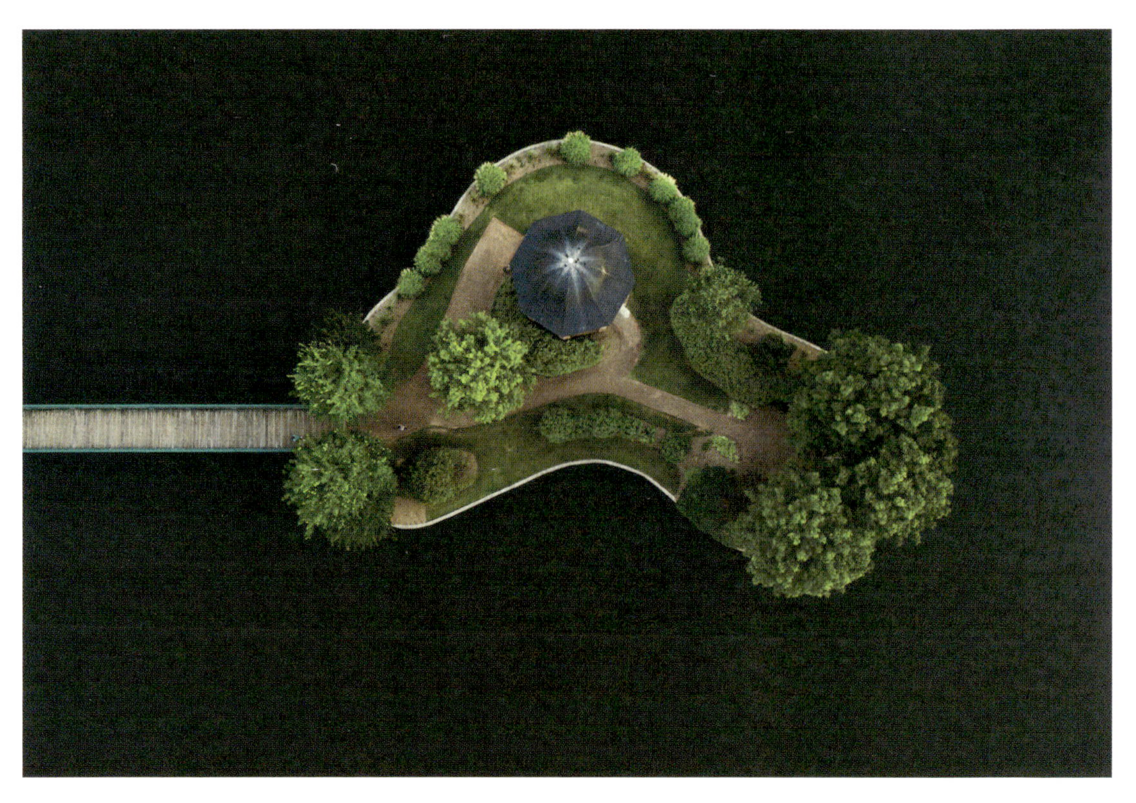

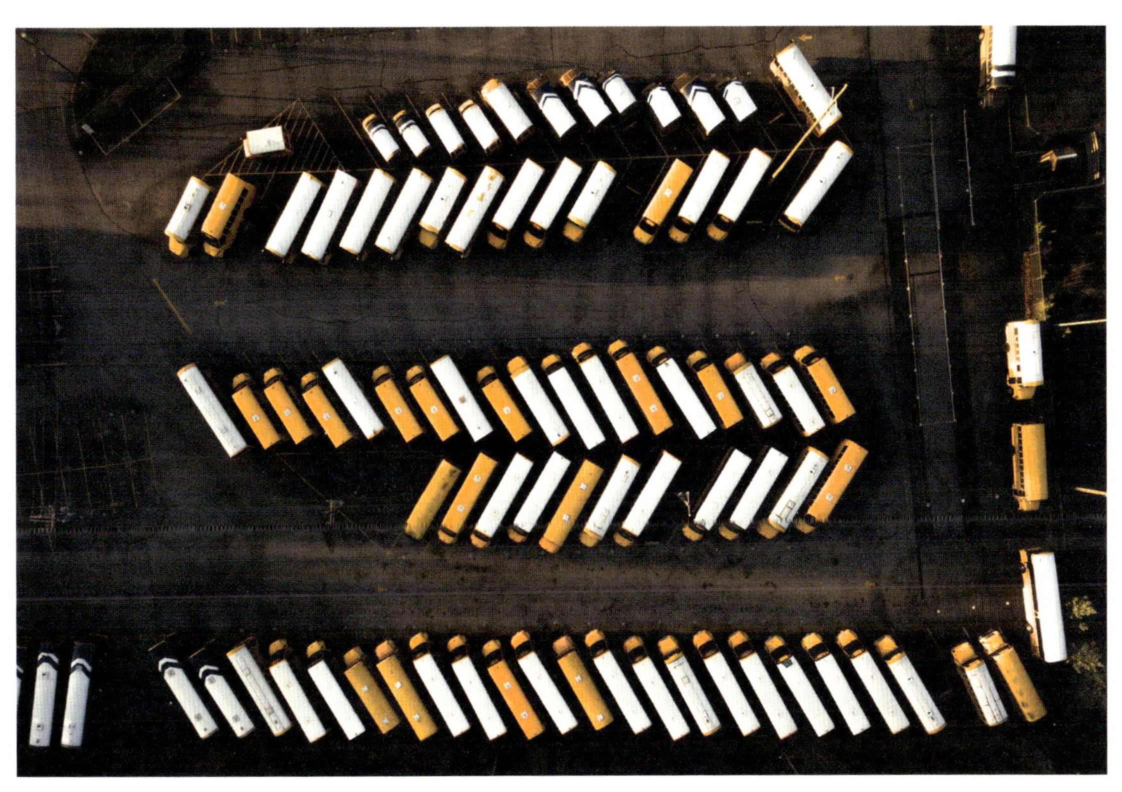

DRAYTON MILLS ELEMENTARY

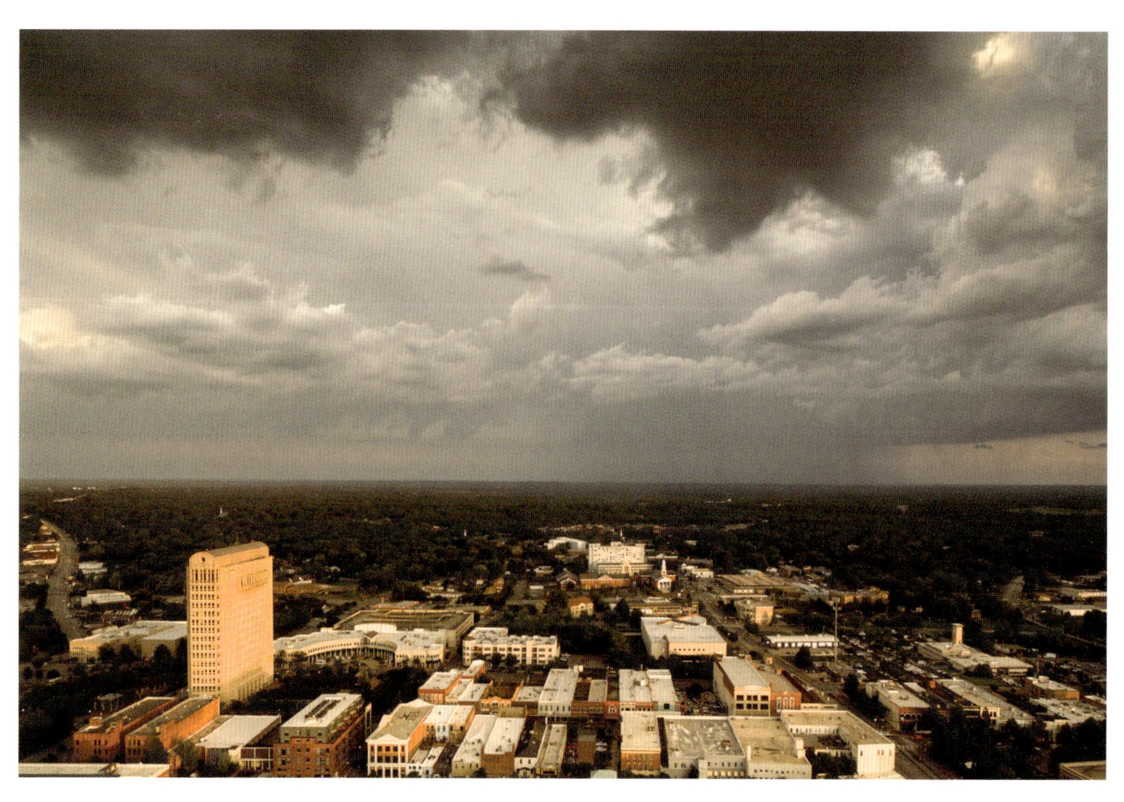

DOWNTOWN SPARTANBURG, BEFORE RAIN |

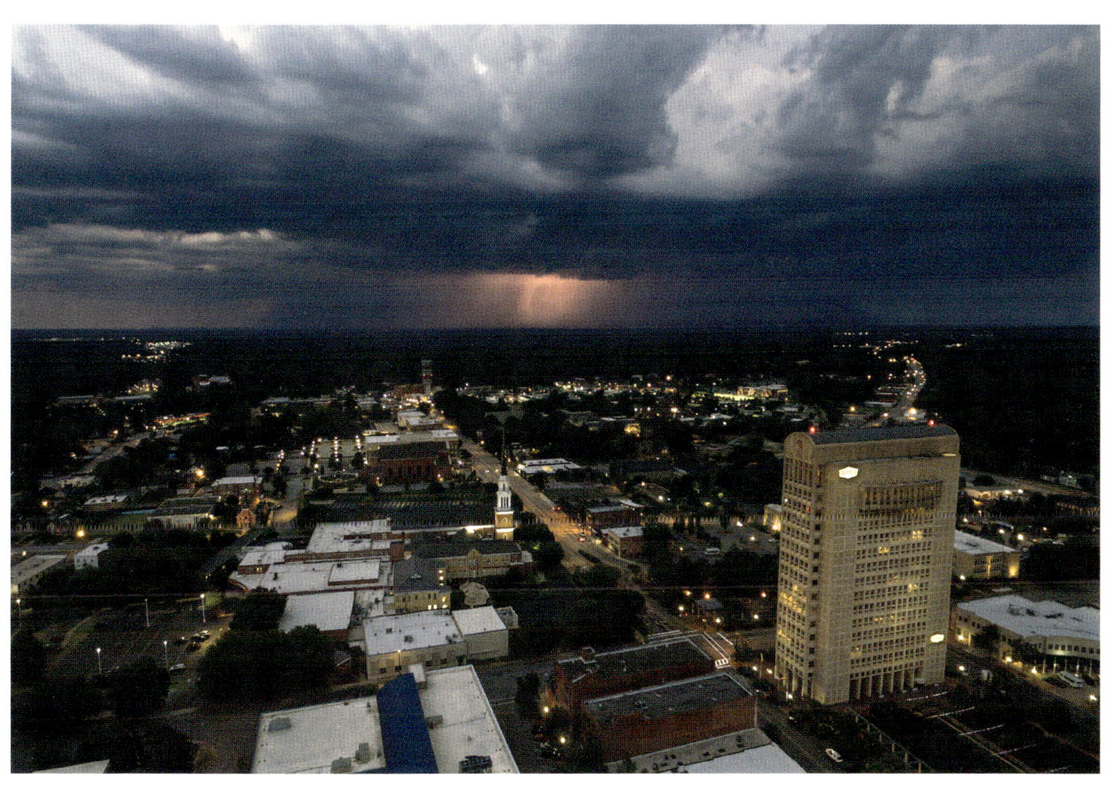

DOWNTOWN SPARTANBURG, THUNDERSTORM

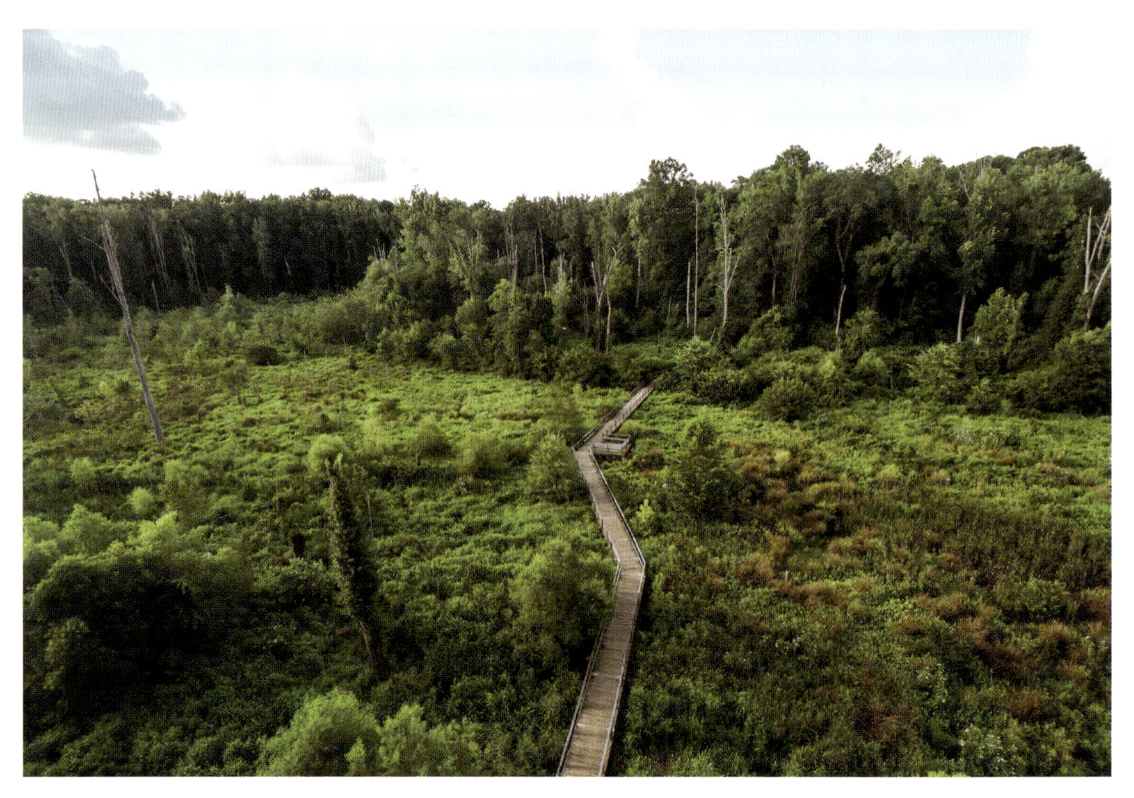

COTTONWOOD TRAIL

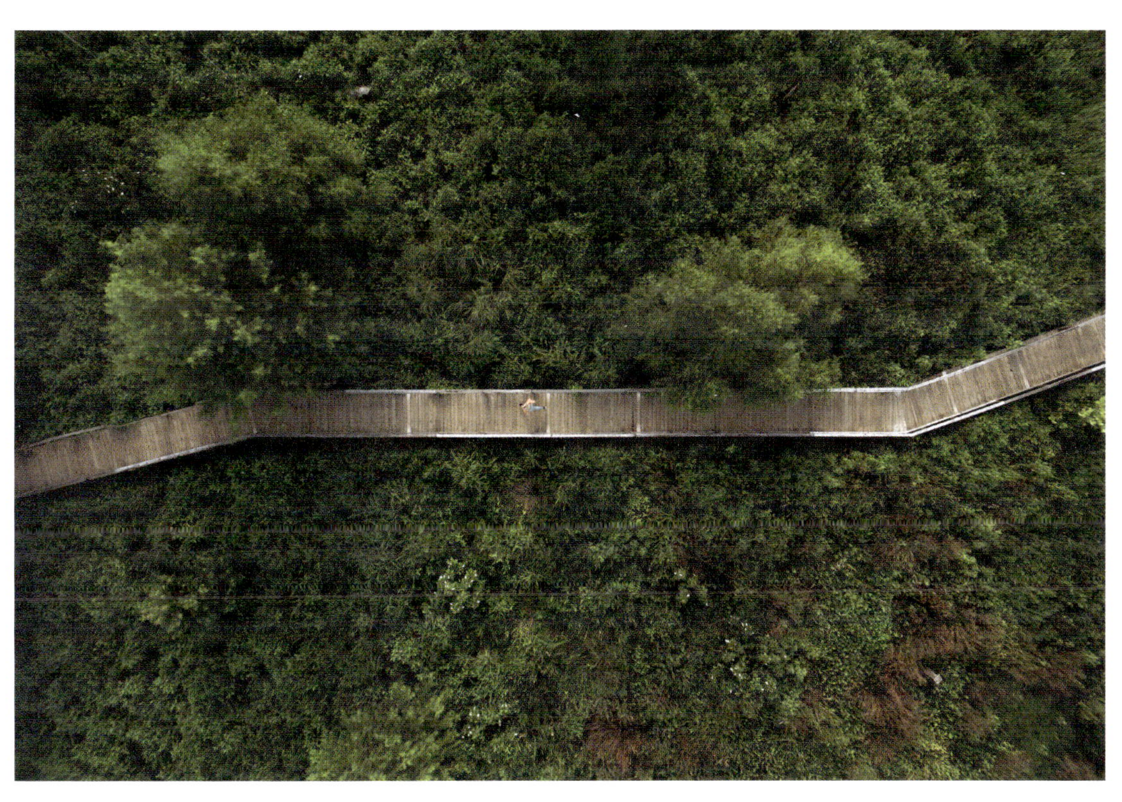

COTTONWOOD RUNNER

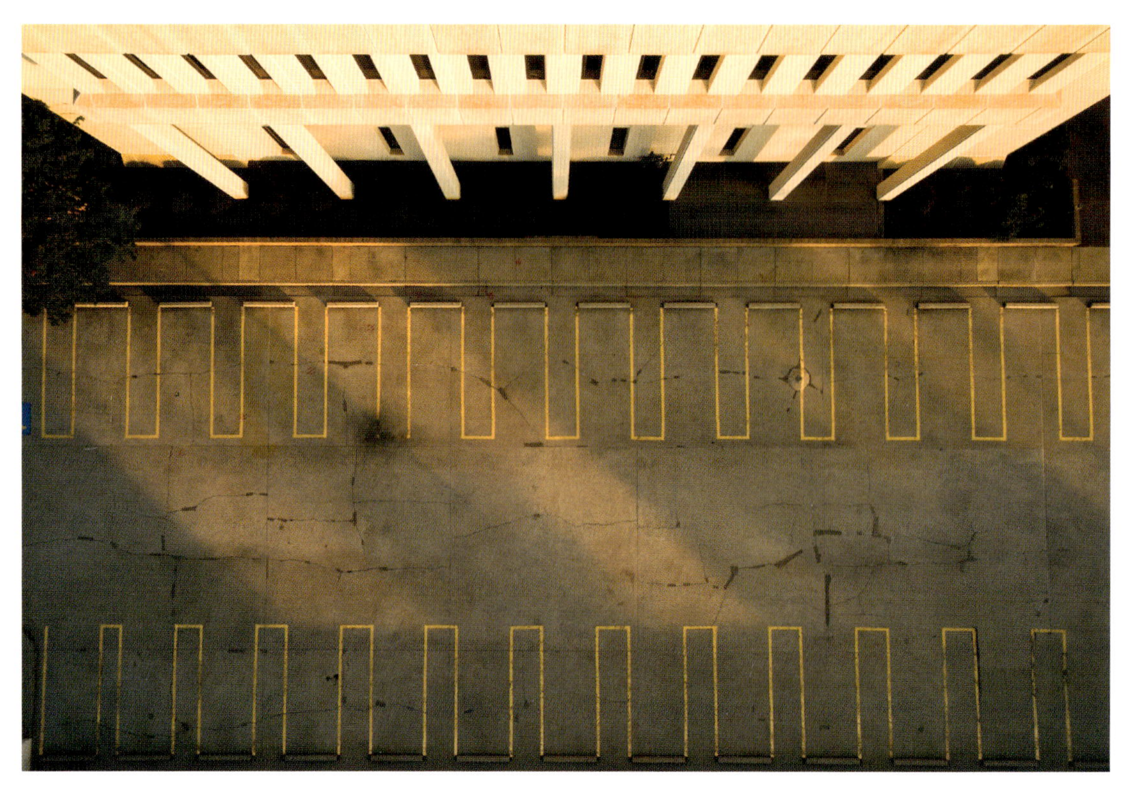

380 E MAIN STREET

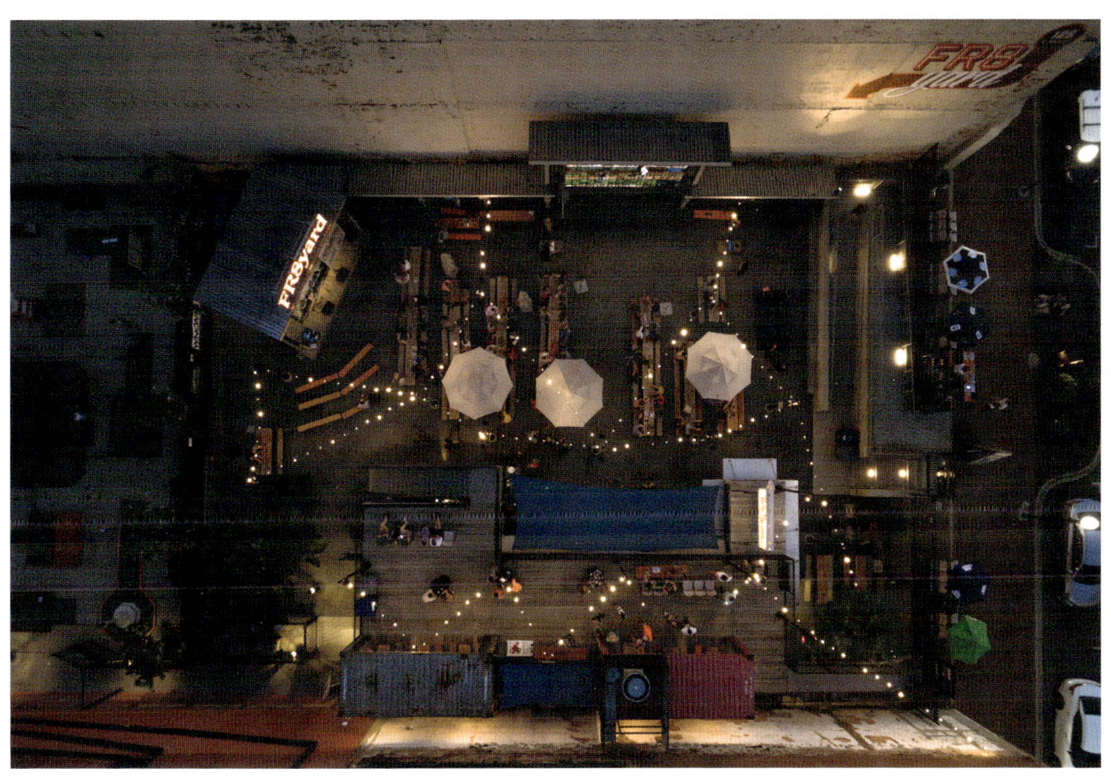

FR8YARD

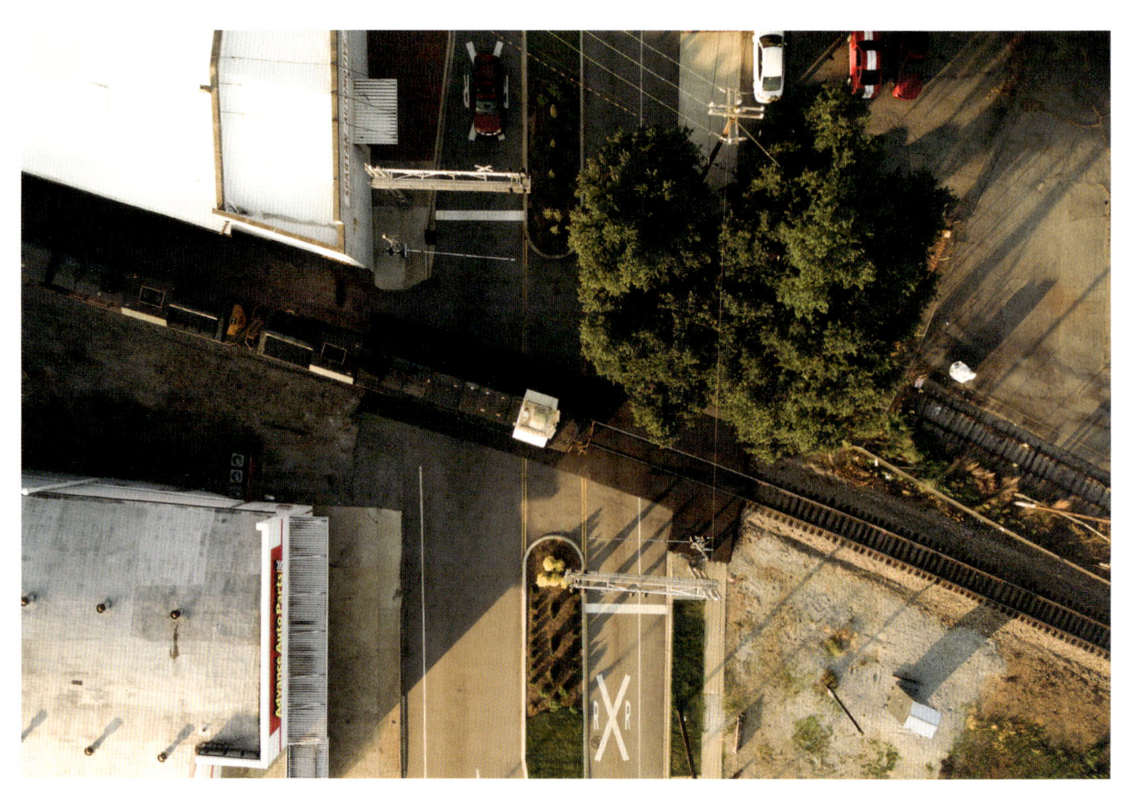

RR X-ING, W MAIN STREET |

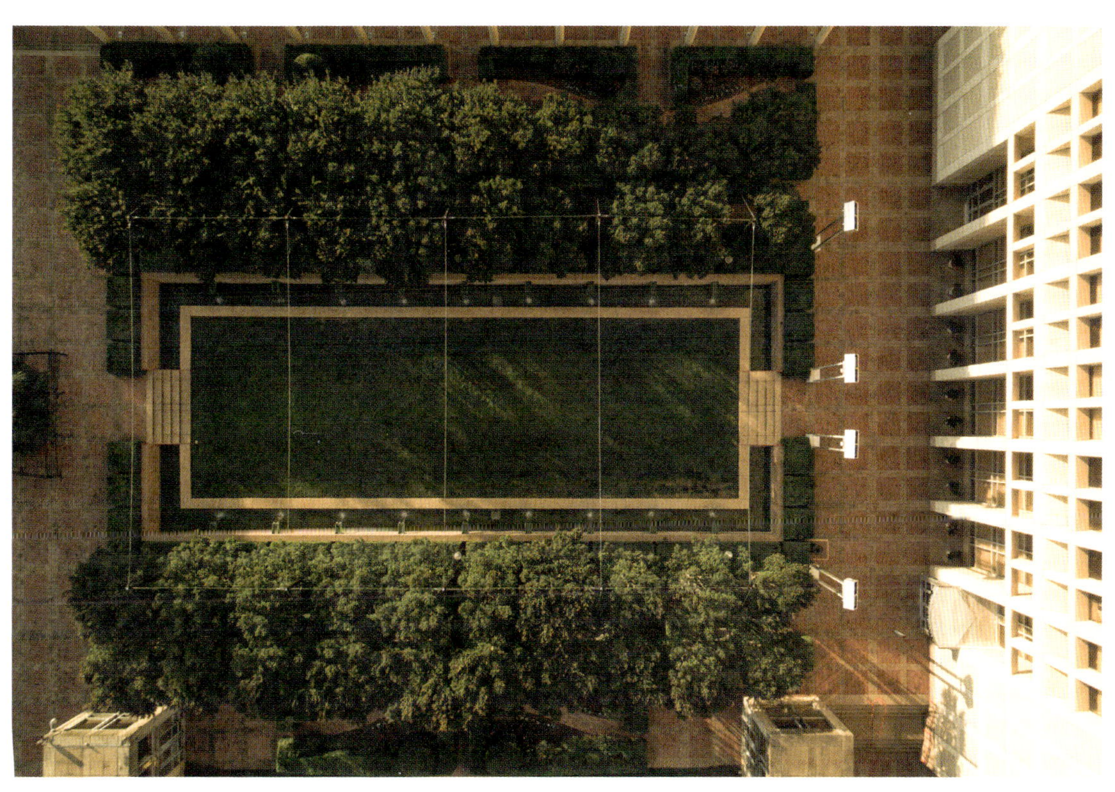

DENNY'S PLAZA

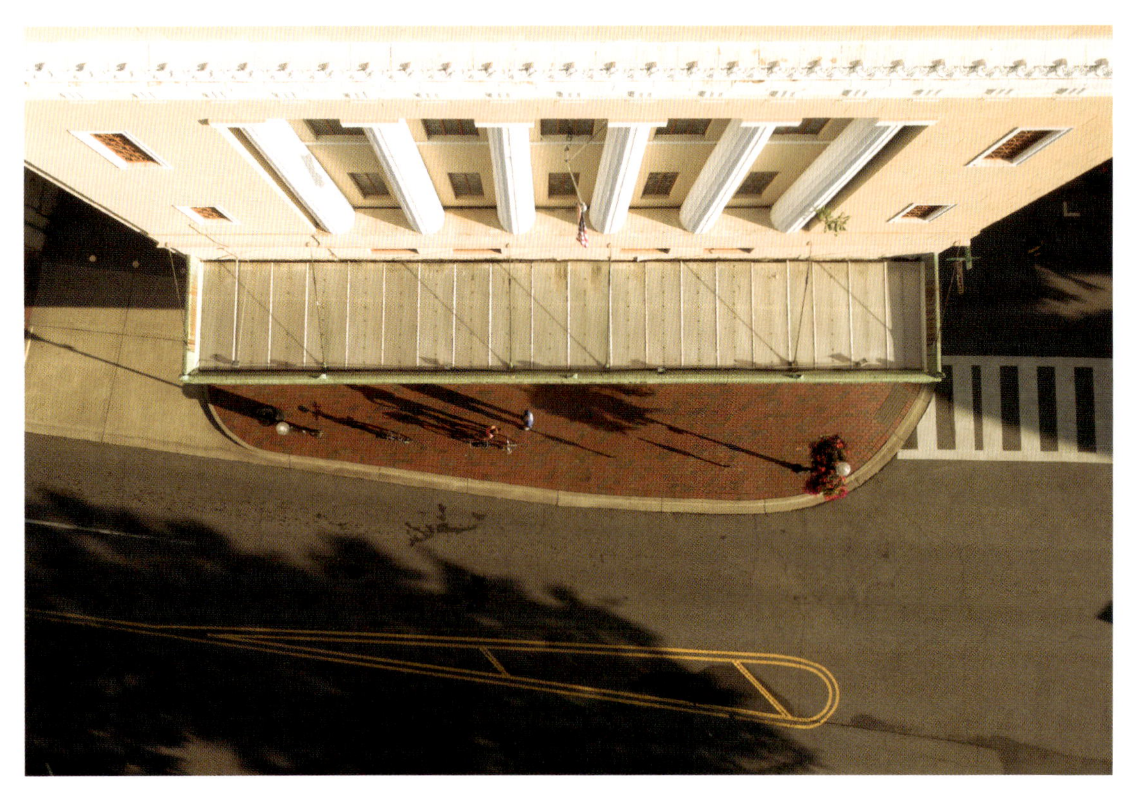

MASONIC TEMPLE |

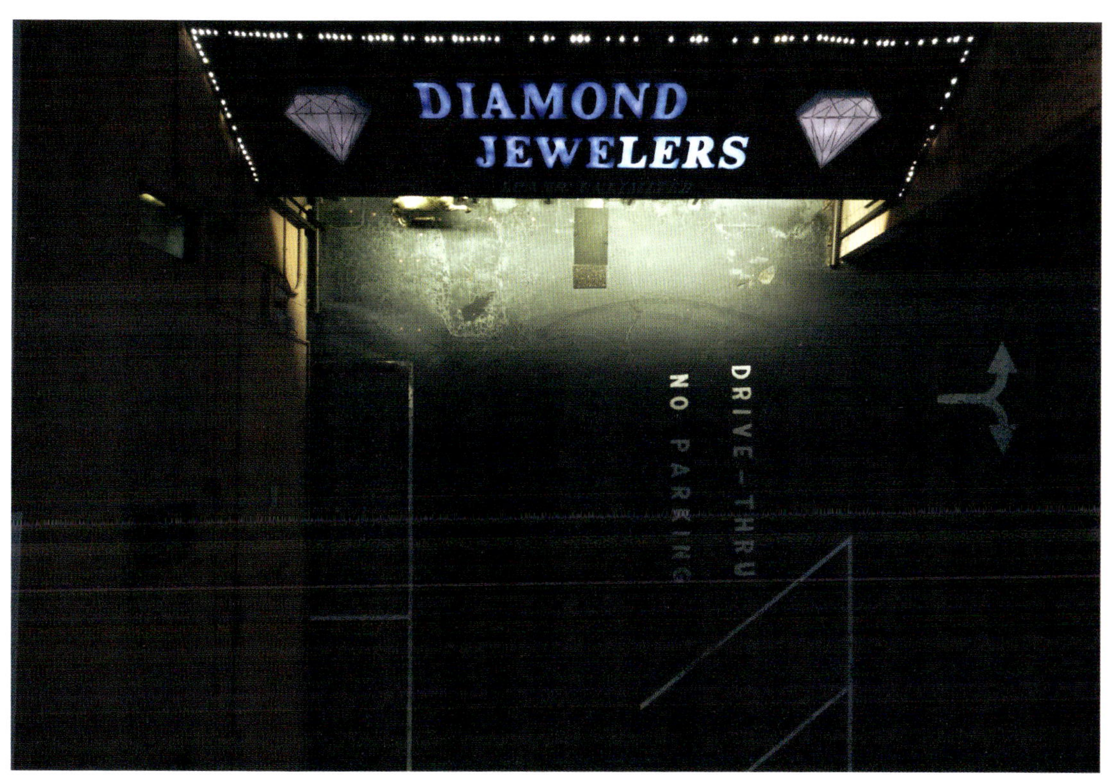

DIAMOND JEWELERS

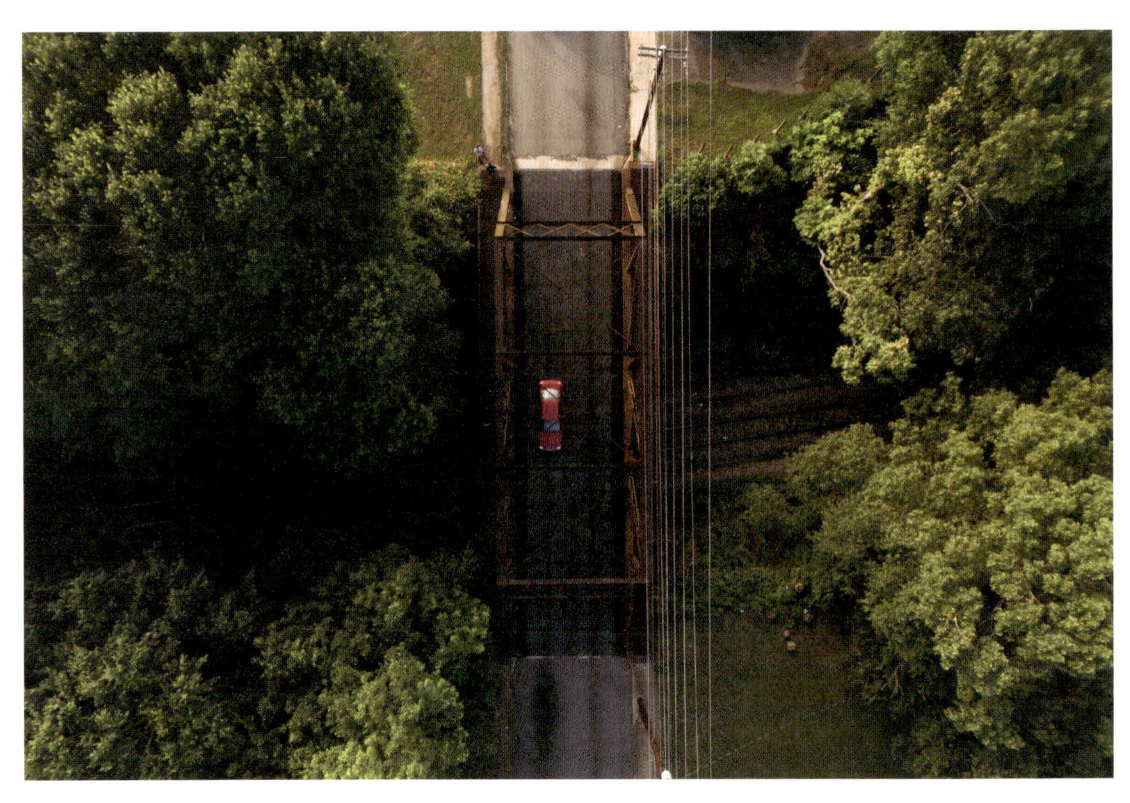

N FOREST STREET BRIDGE |

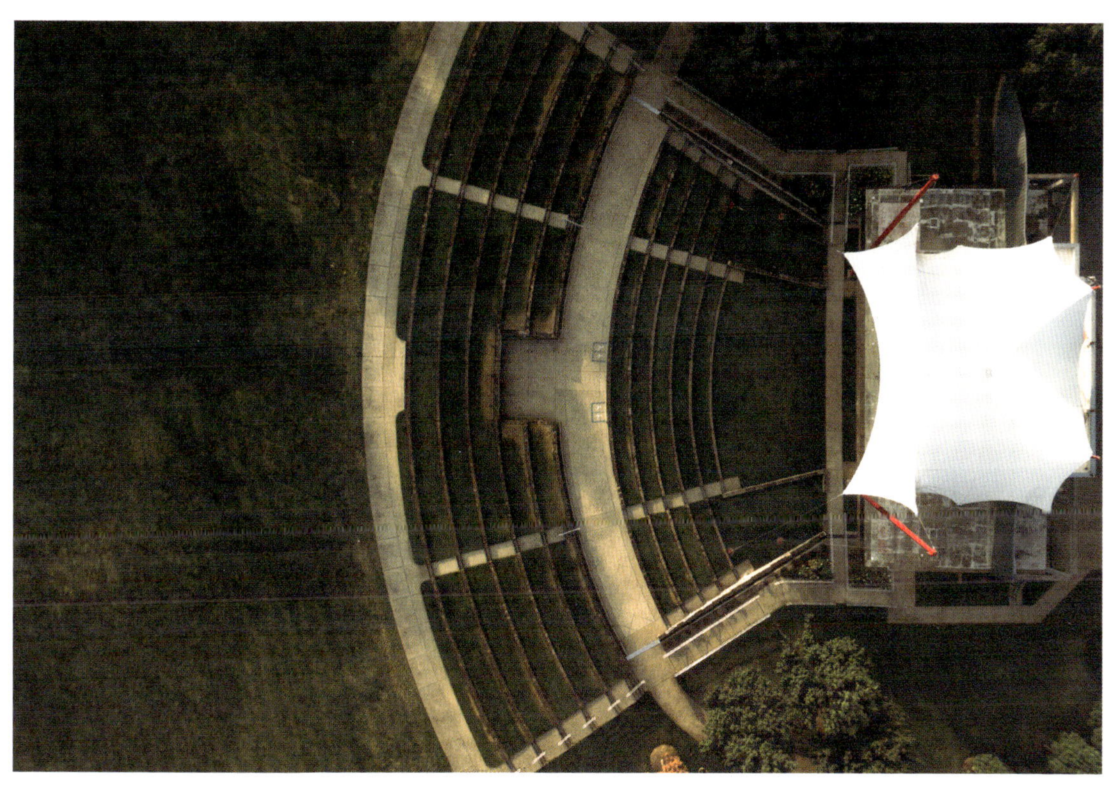

BARNET PARK

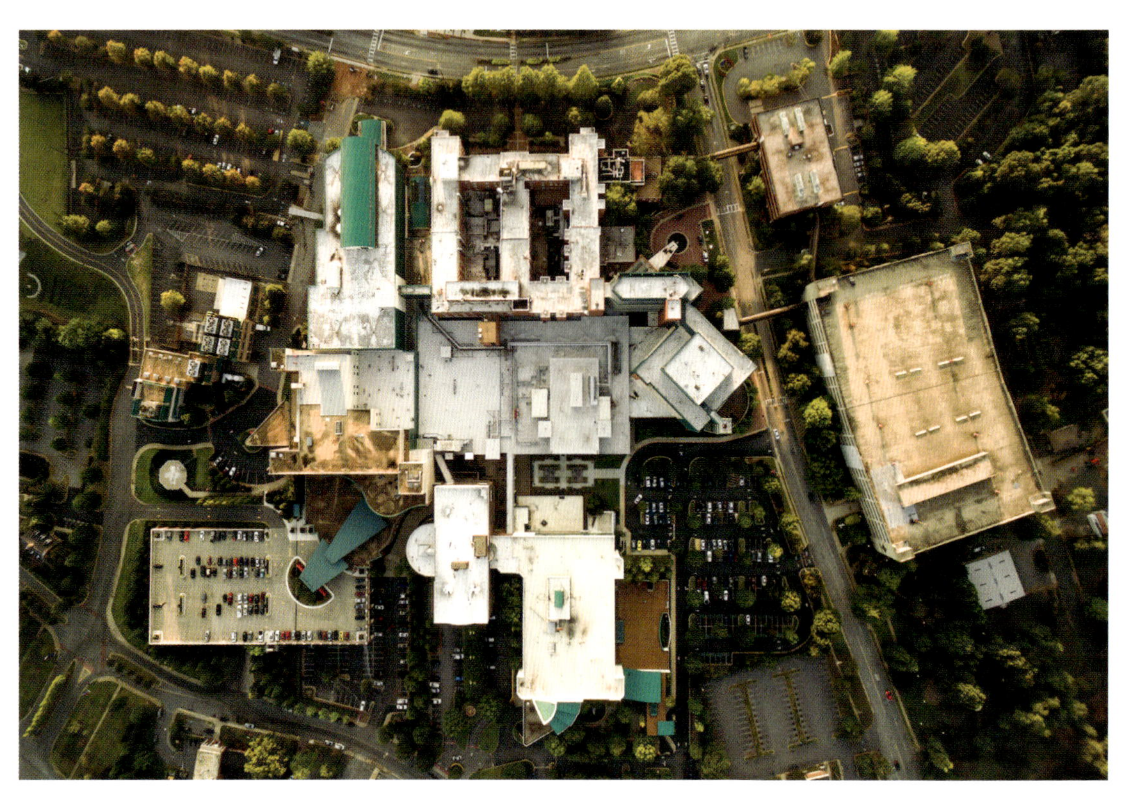

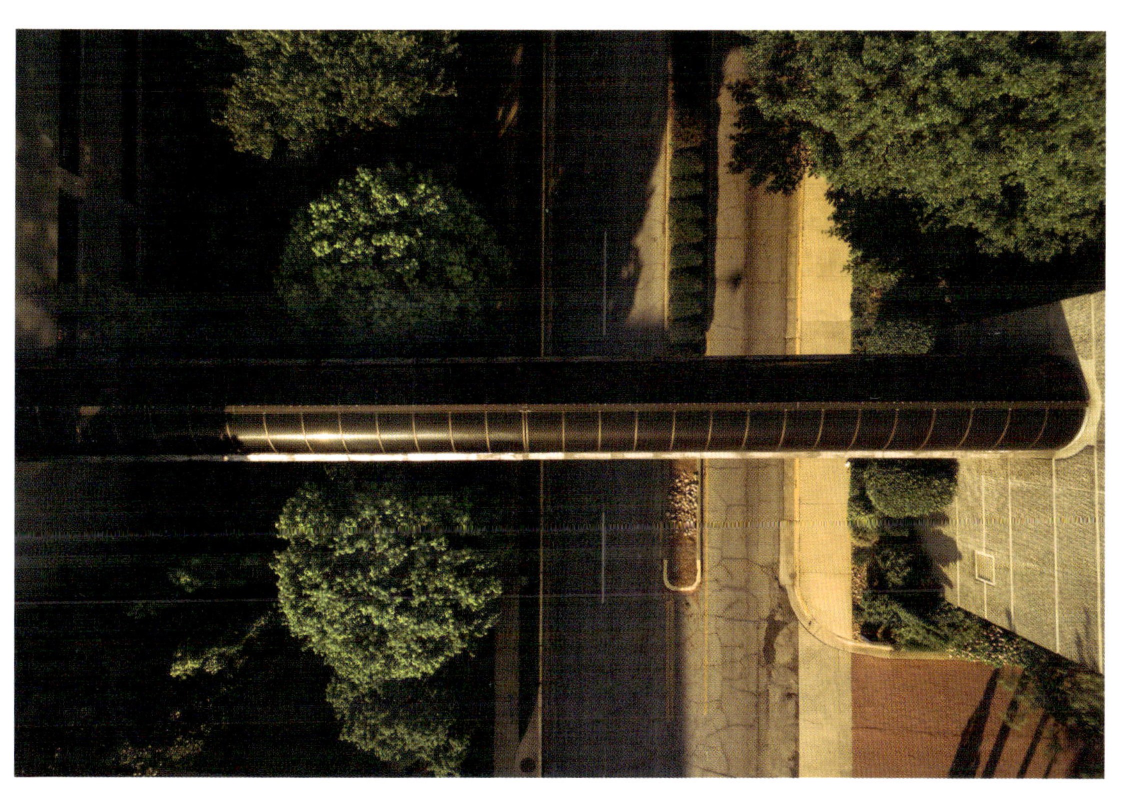

HUMAN HAMSTER TUBE, E WOOD STREET

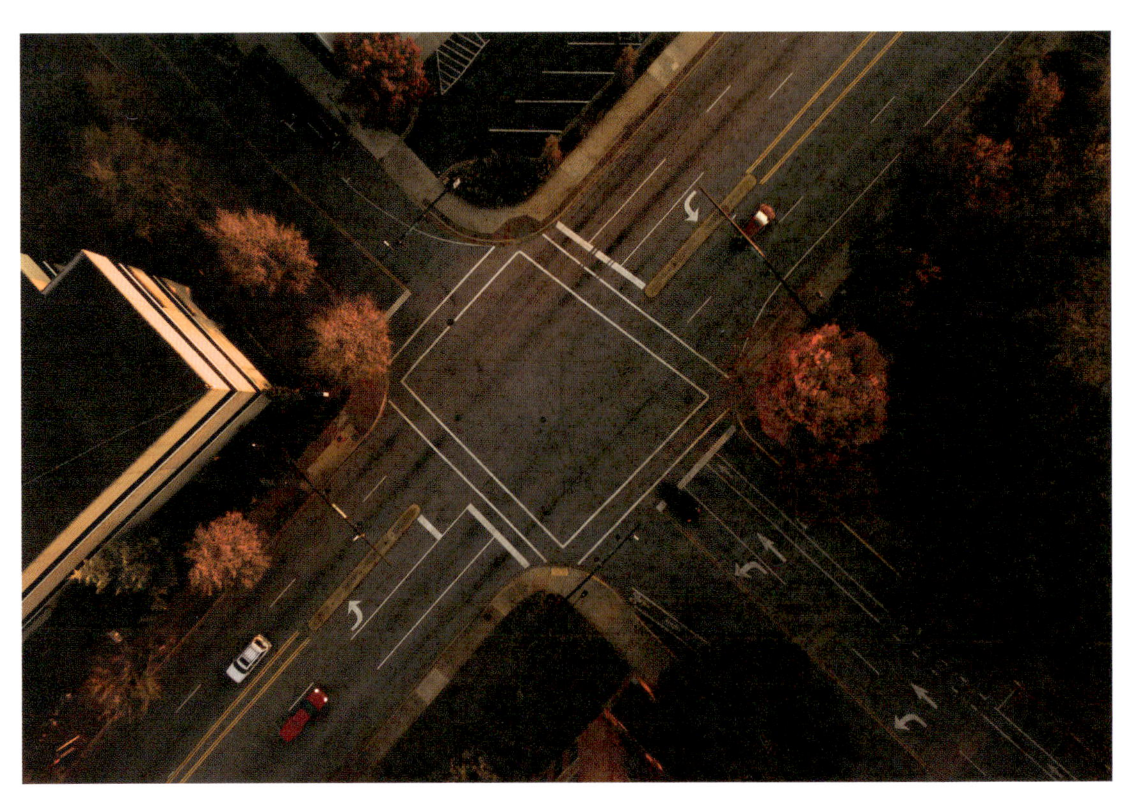

SAINT JOHN AND MAGNOLIA |

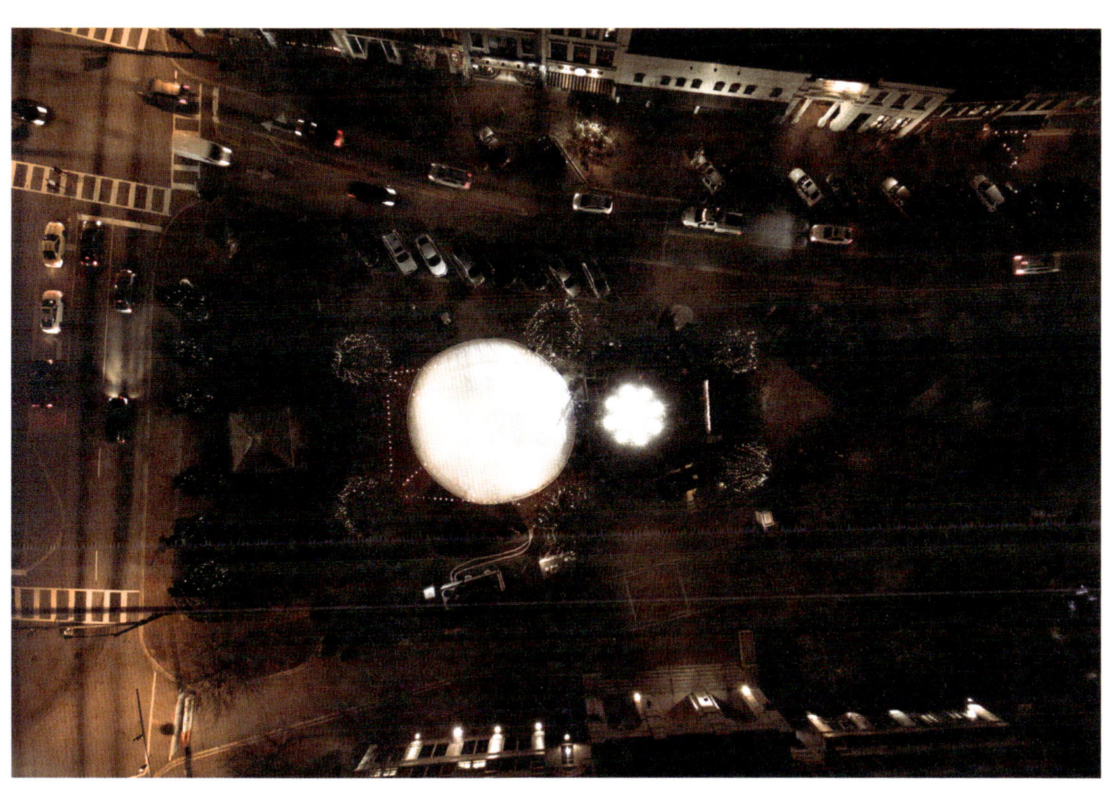

| SKATING ON THE SQUARE

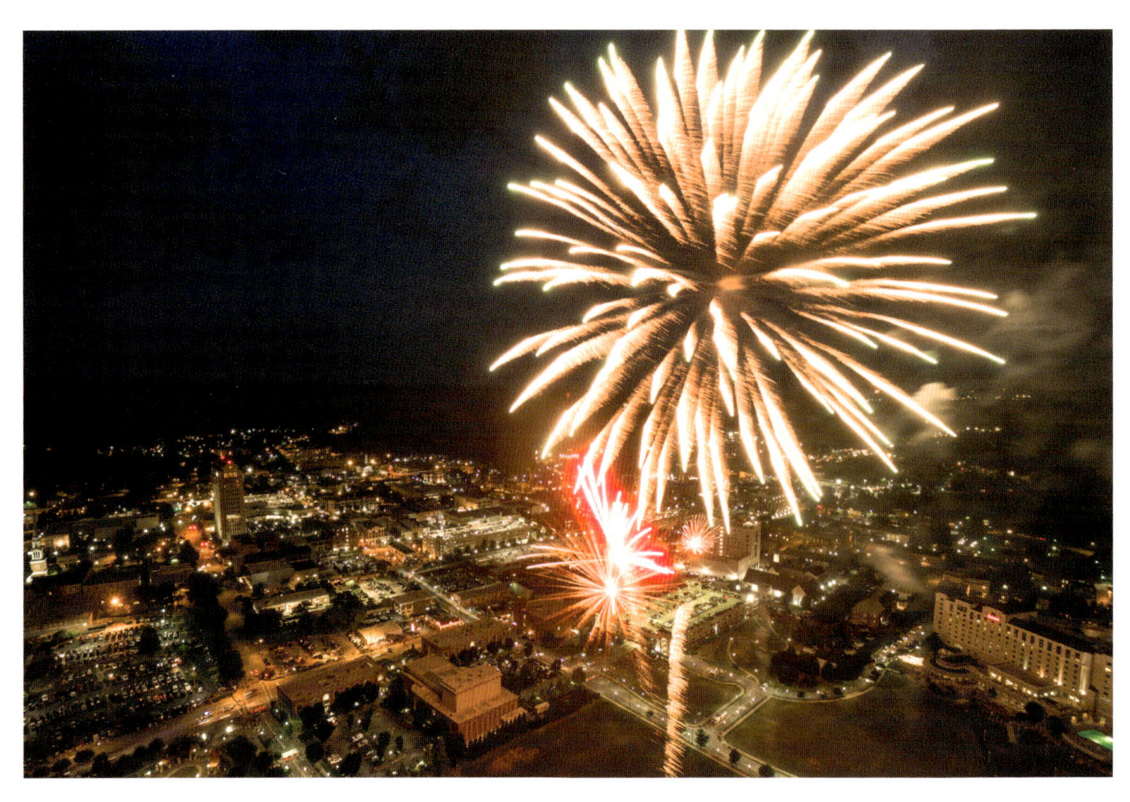

RED, WHITE, AND BOOM |

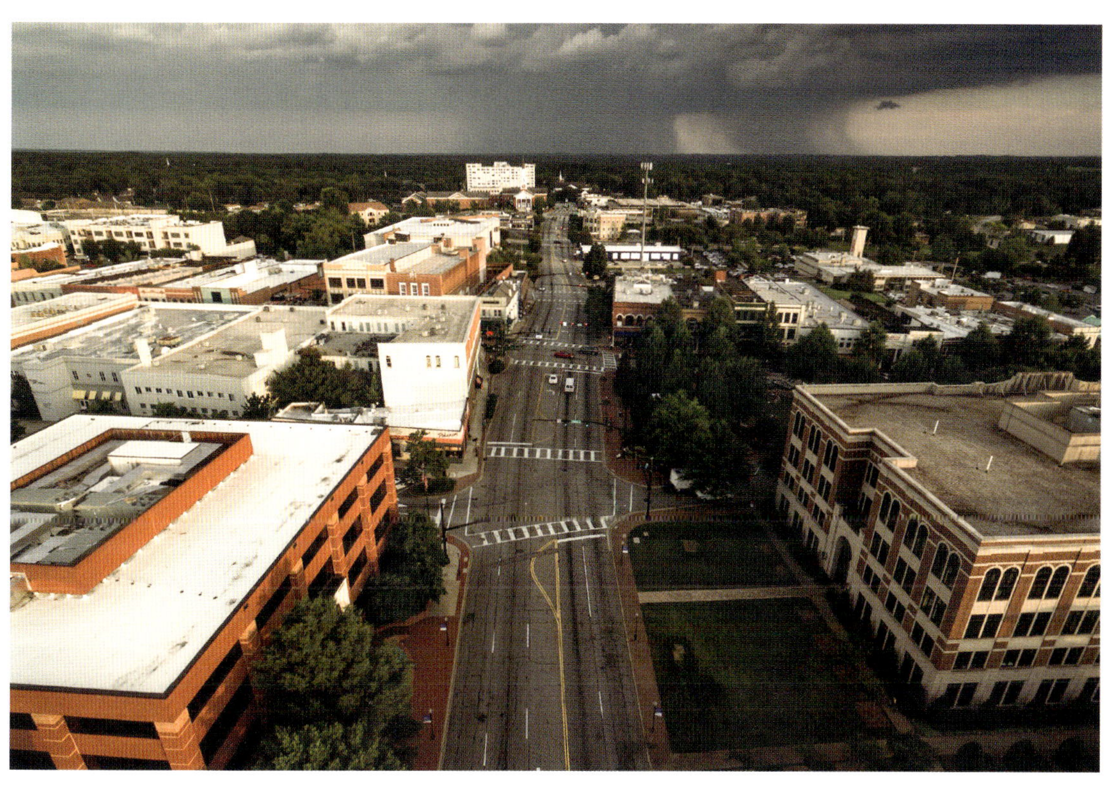

CHURCH STREET

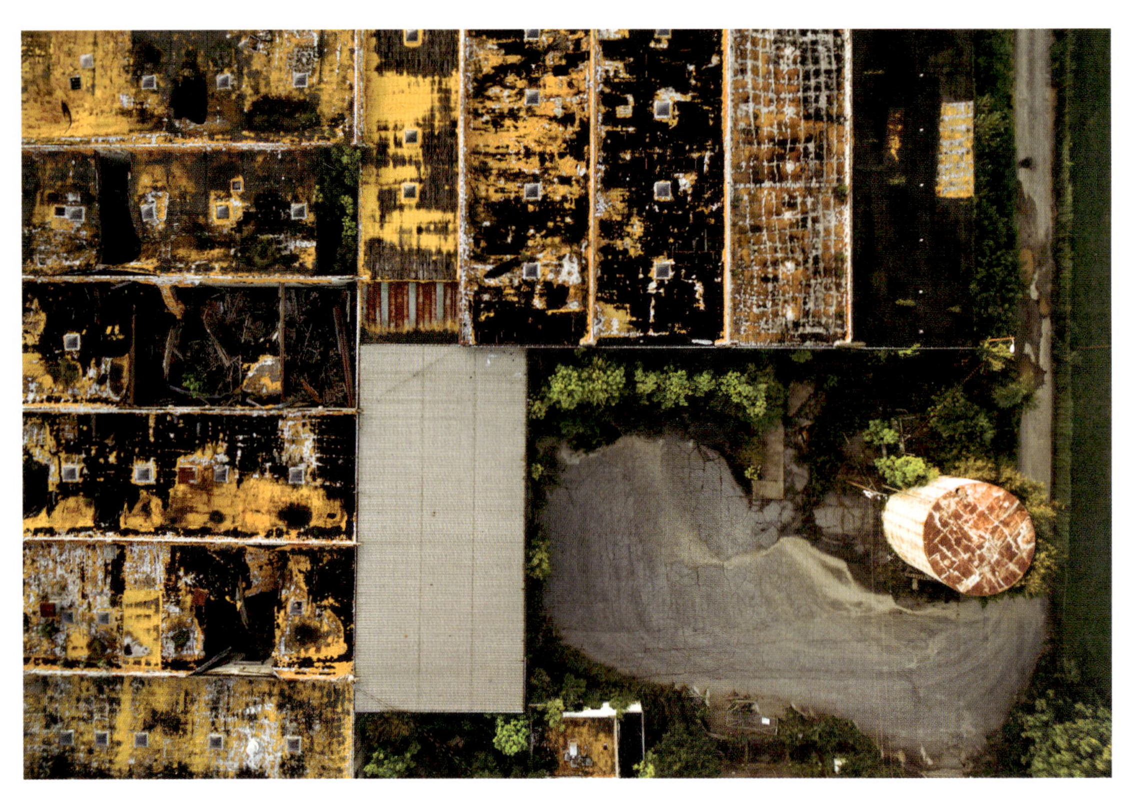

ADEN BONDED WAREHOUSE CO |

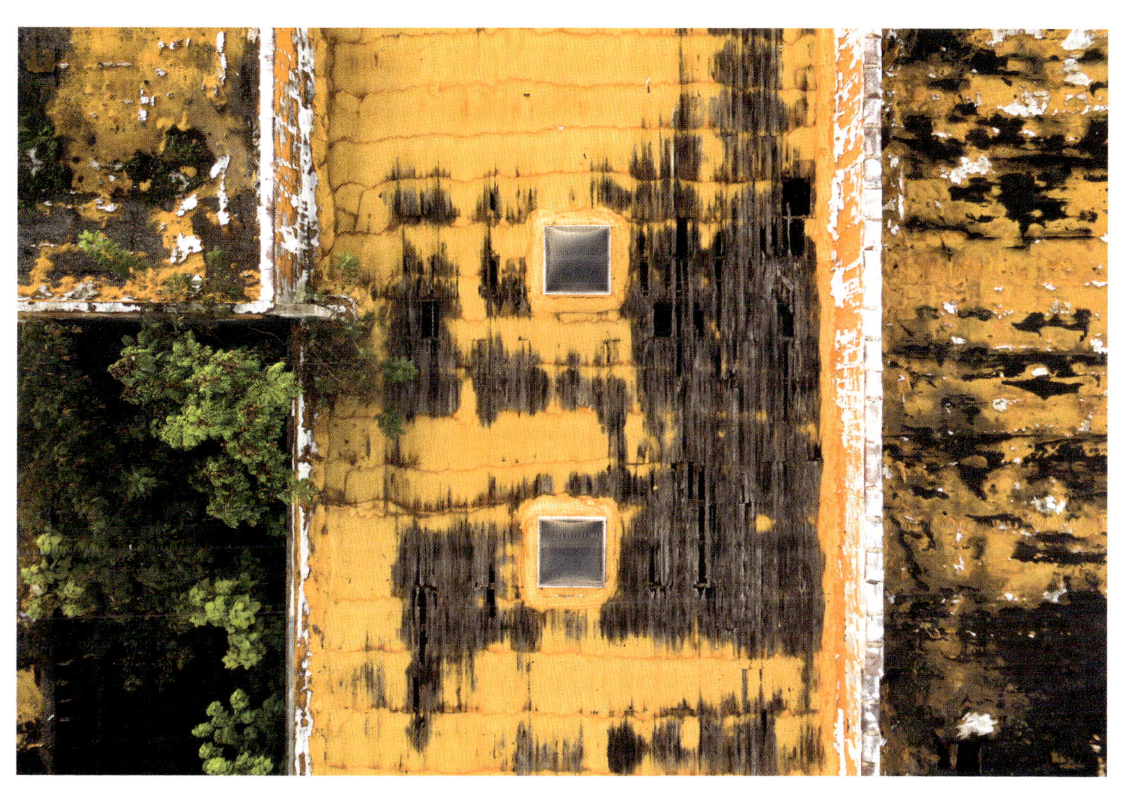

YELLOW ROOF

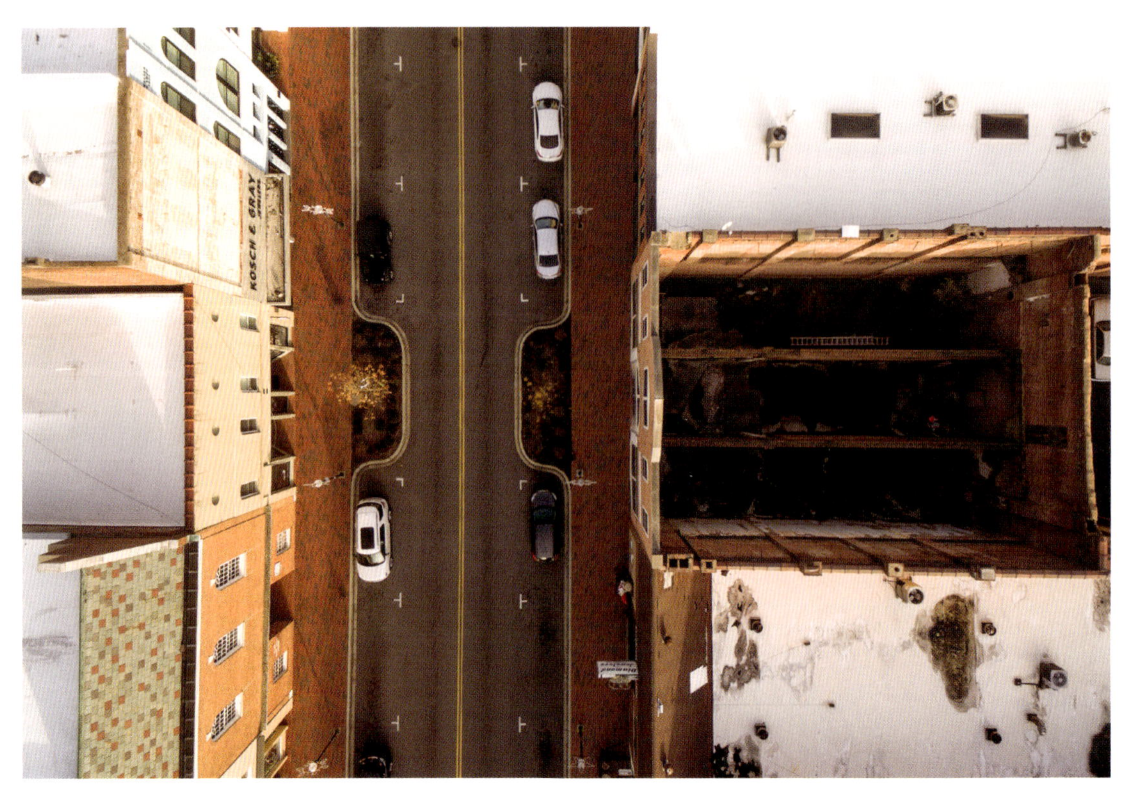

163 E MAIN ST |

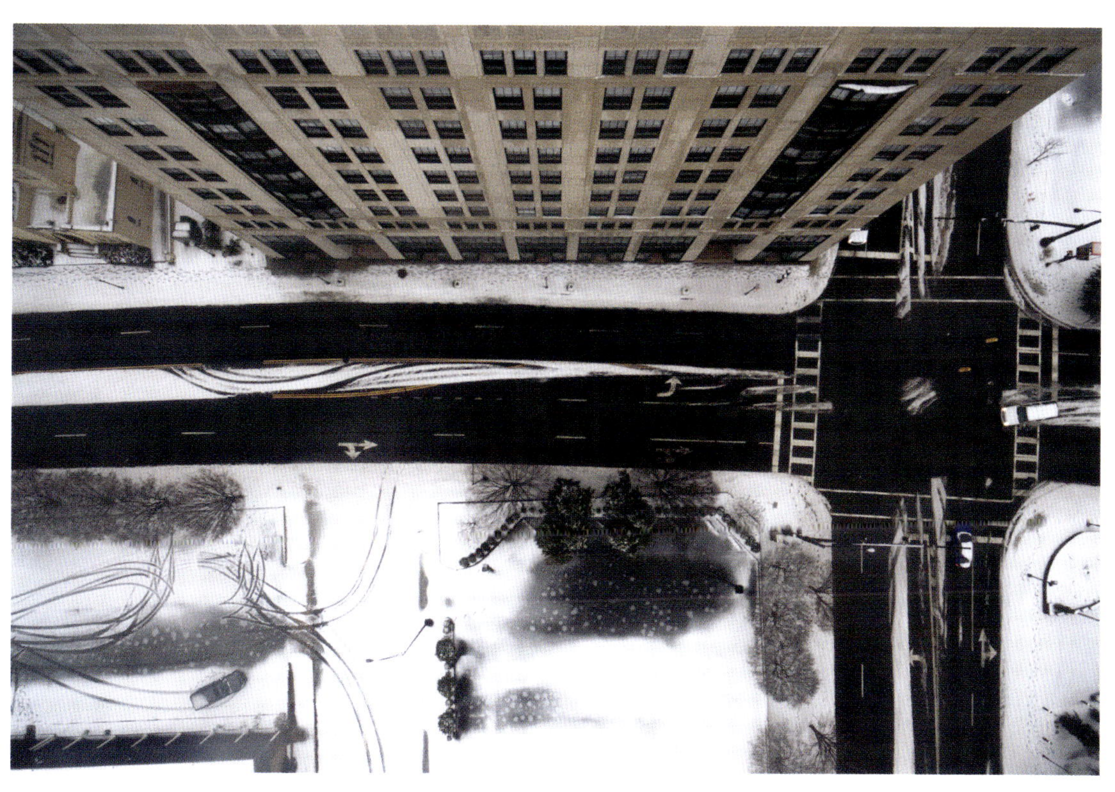

| MONTGOMERY BUILDING

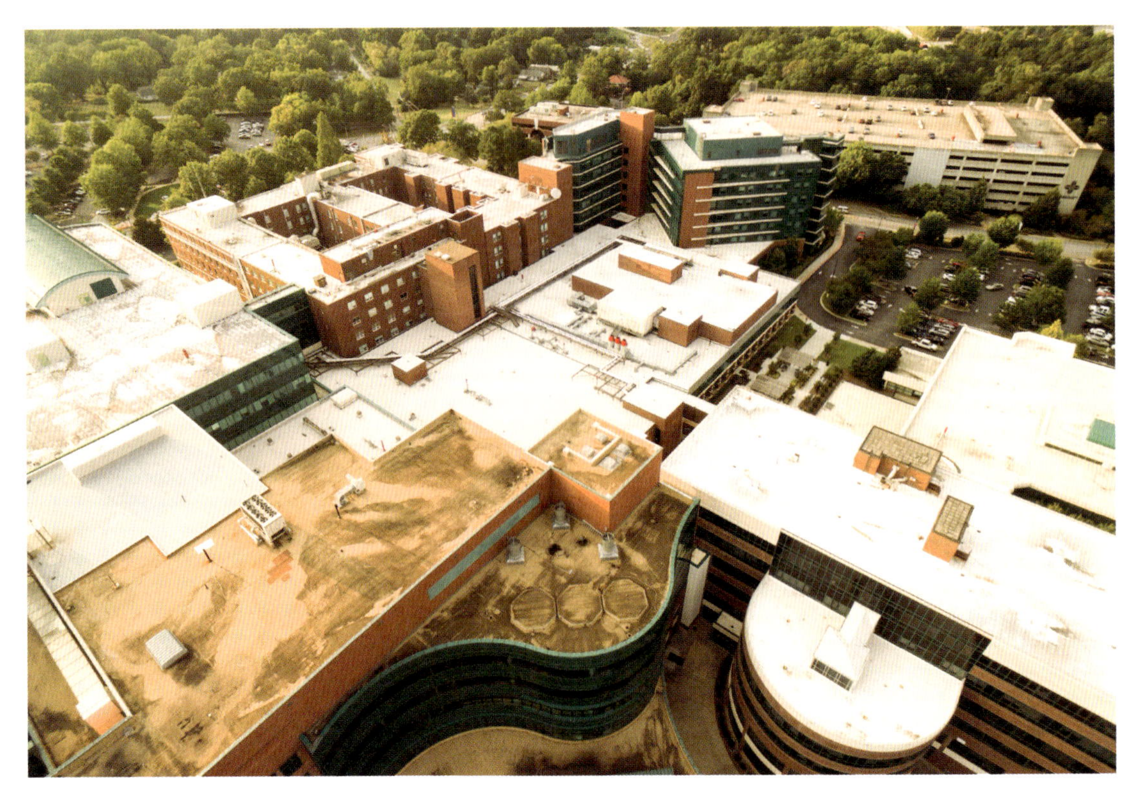

SPARTANBURG REGIONAL |

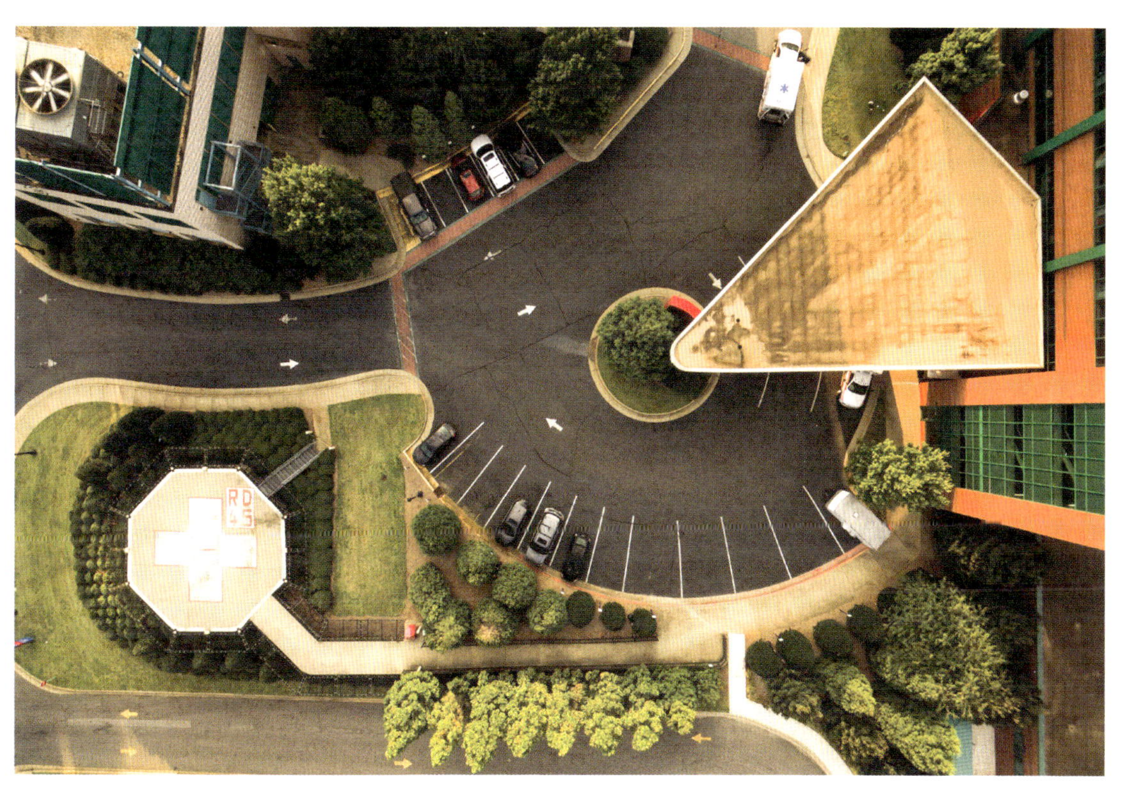

| SPARTANBURG REGIONAL WEST WING

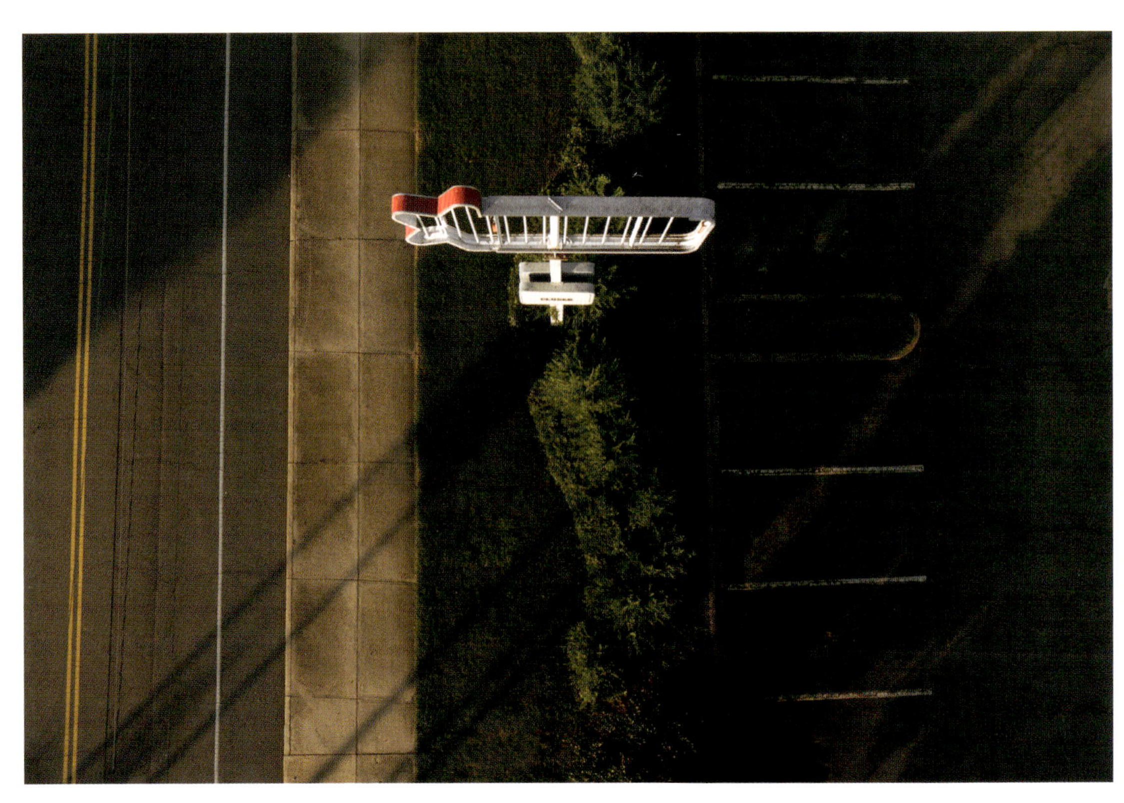

HARDEE'S SIGN, W MAIN STREET |

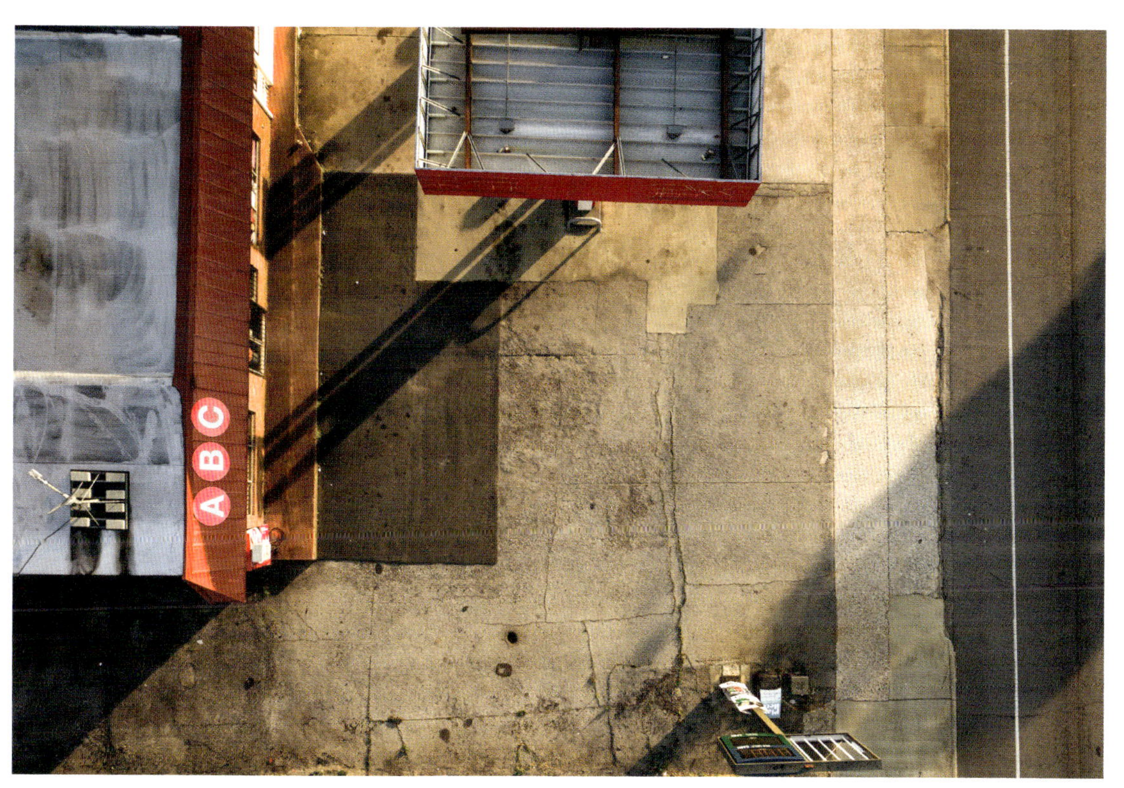

| ABC STORE, W MAIN STREET

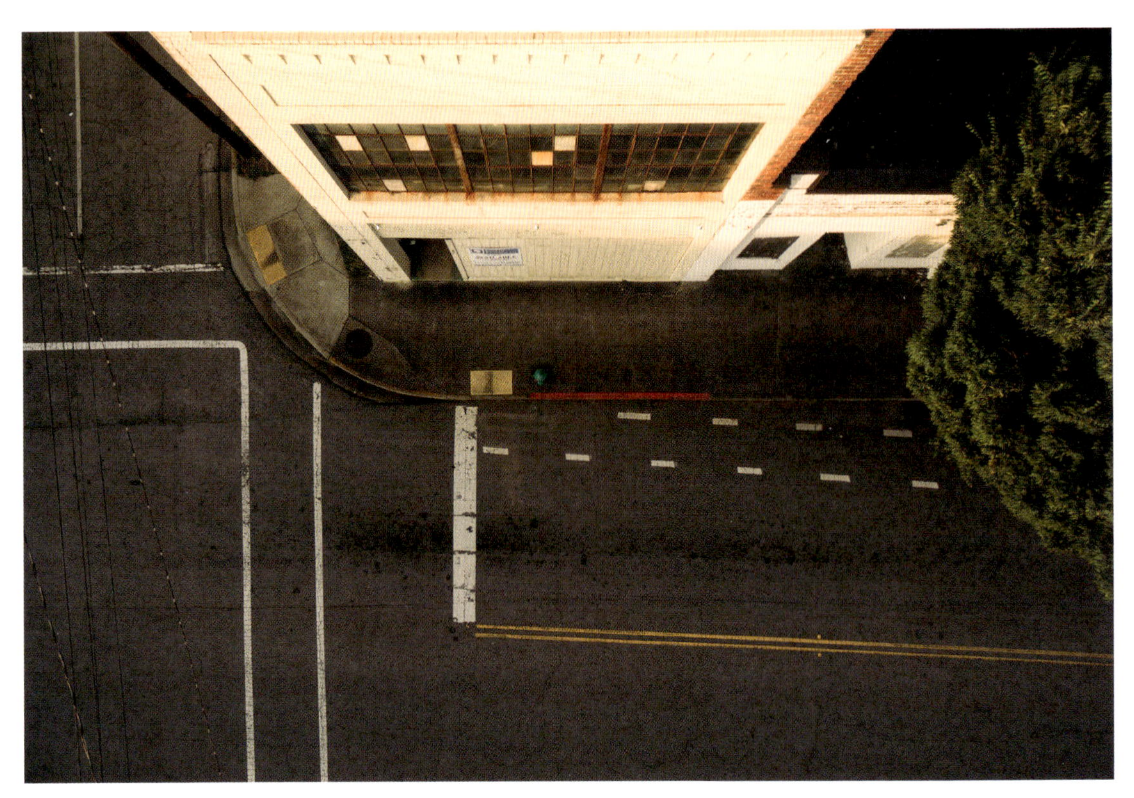

MAGNOLIA STREET PUB |

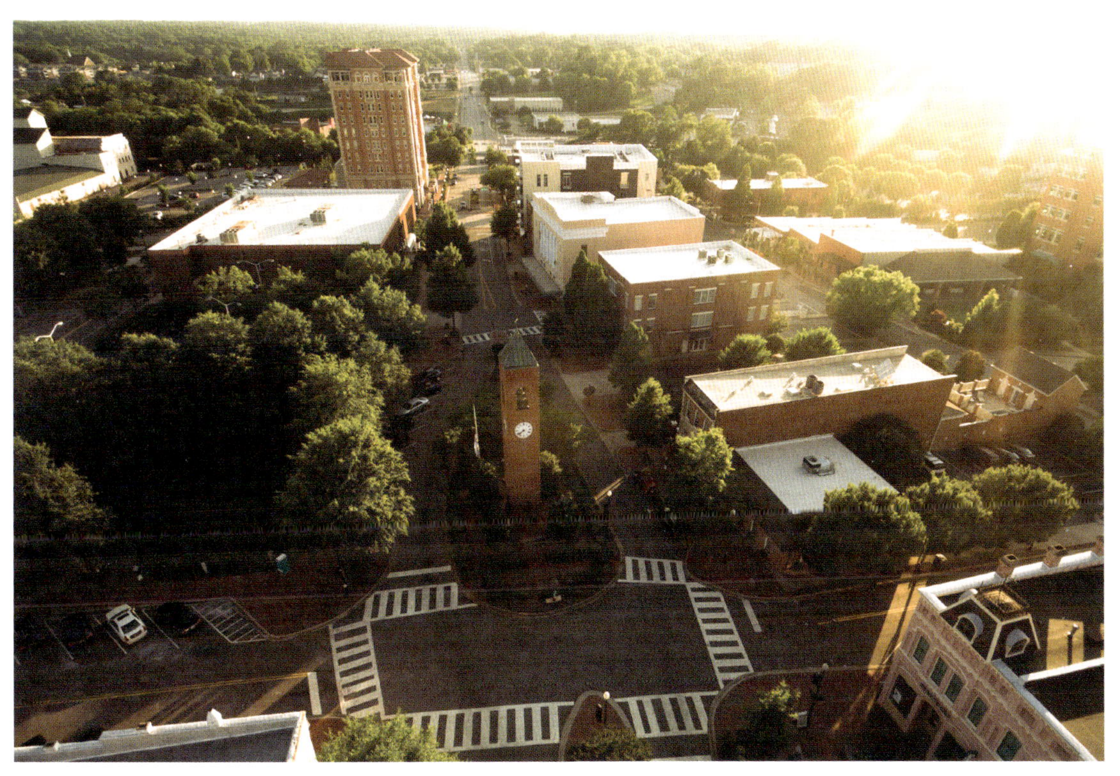

| CLOCK TOWER, SUNDAY EVENING

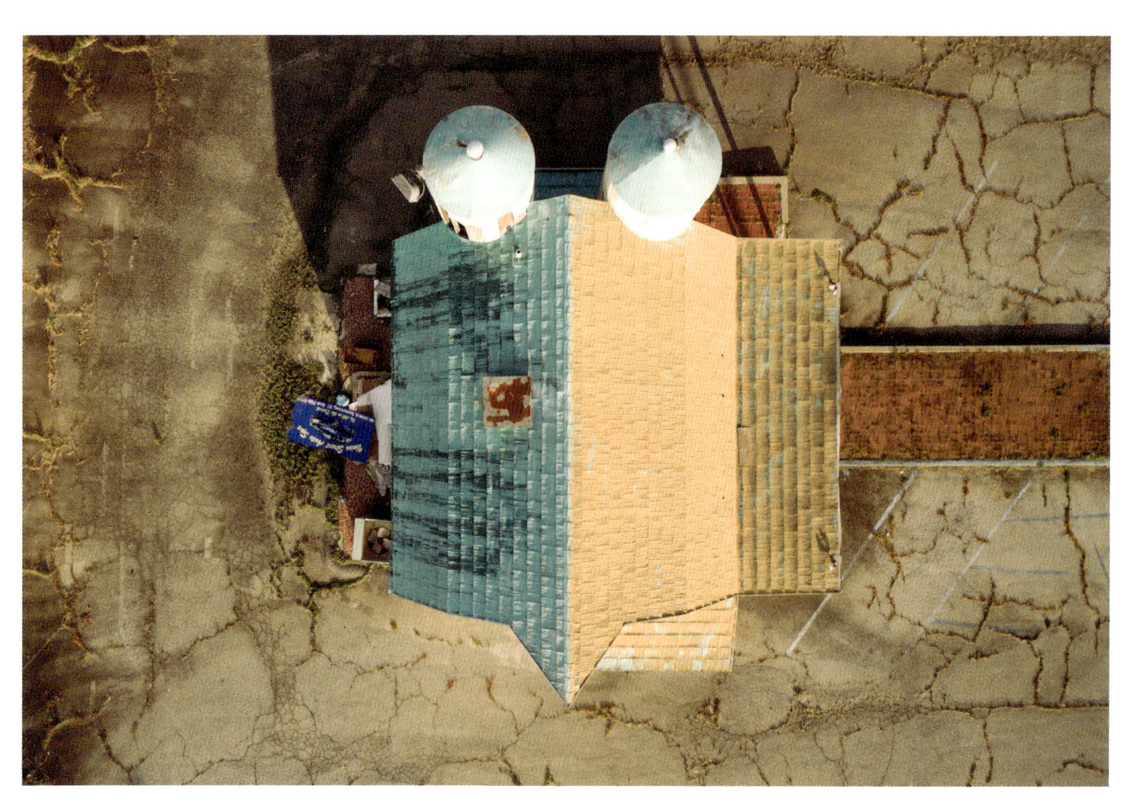

SECOND CHANCE AUTO MALL, UNION STREET |

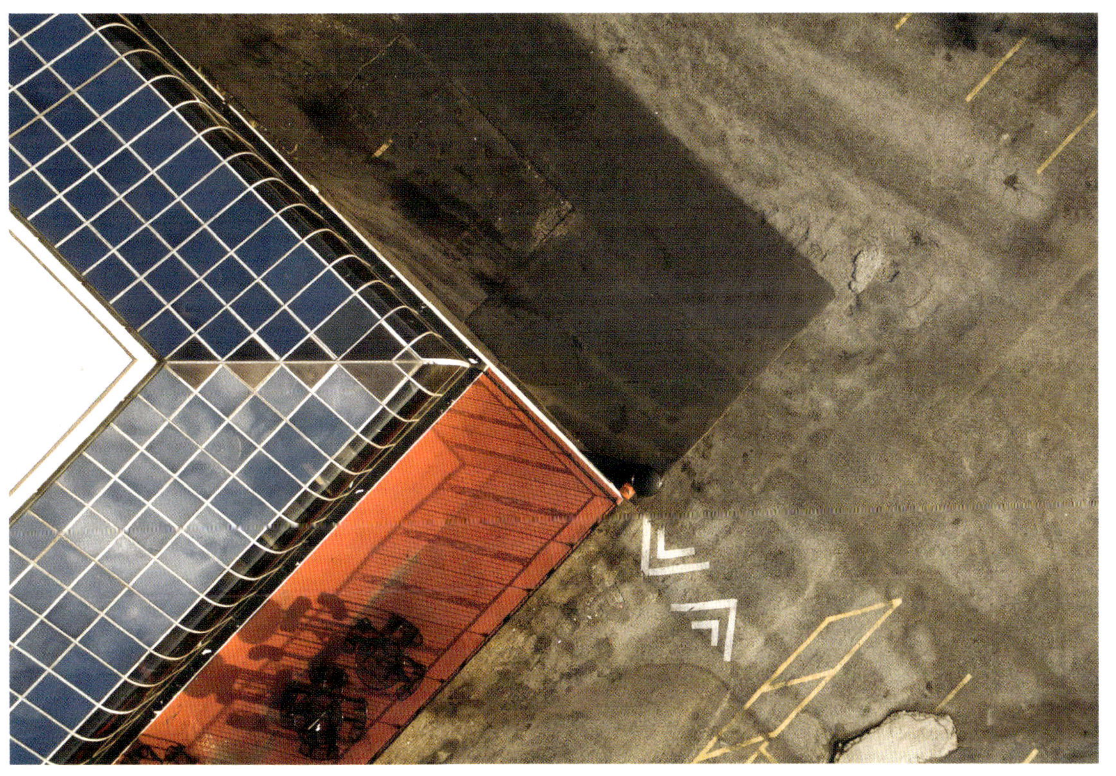

THE BEACON

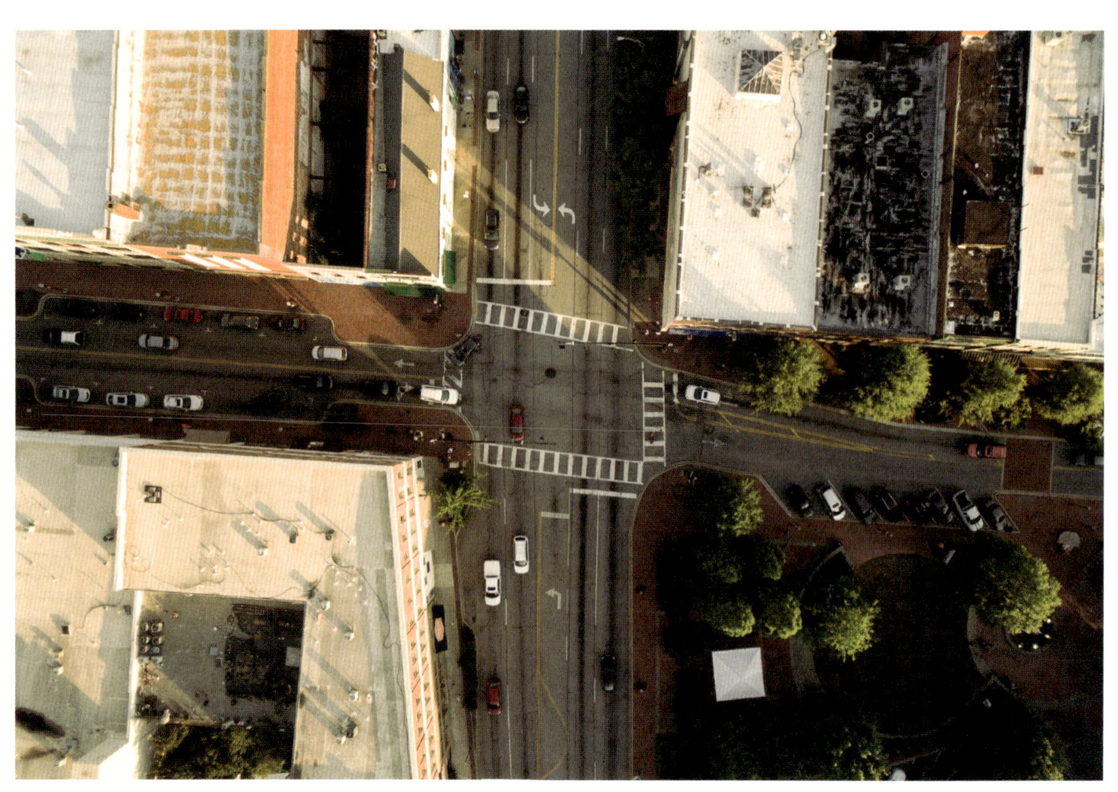

CHURCH AND MAIN |

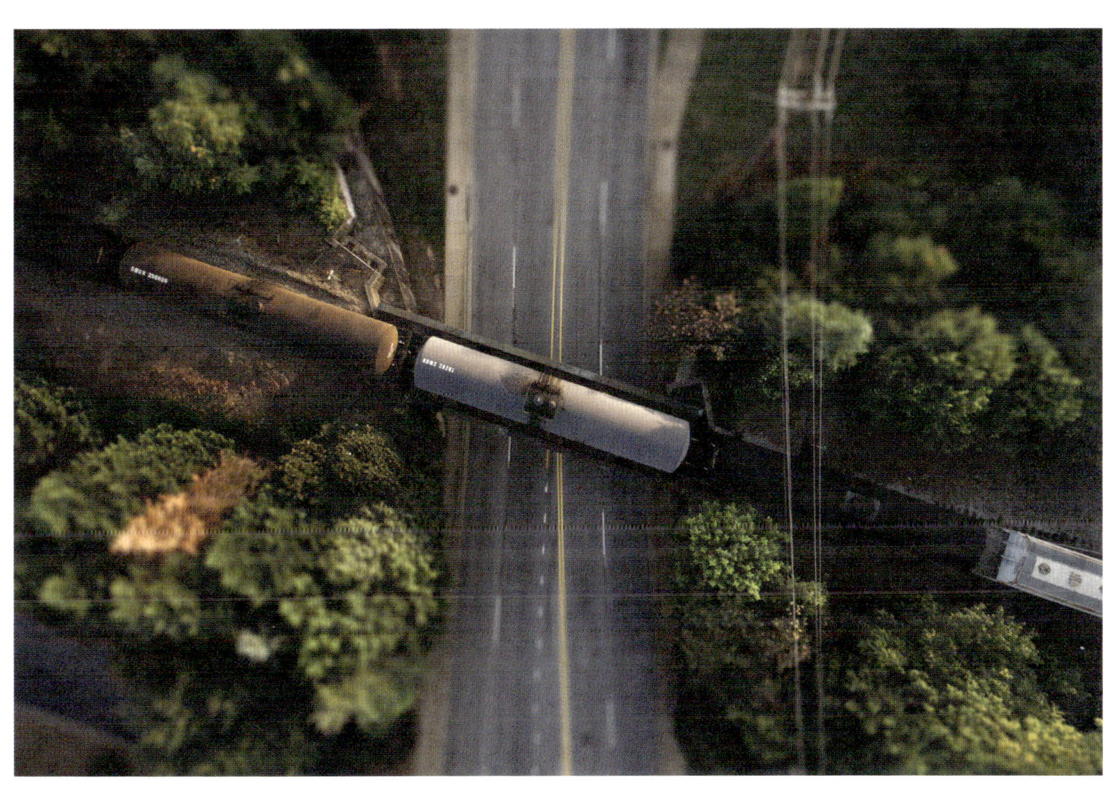

W SAINT JOHN TRAIN

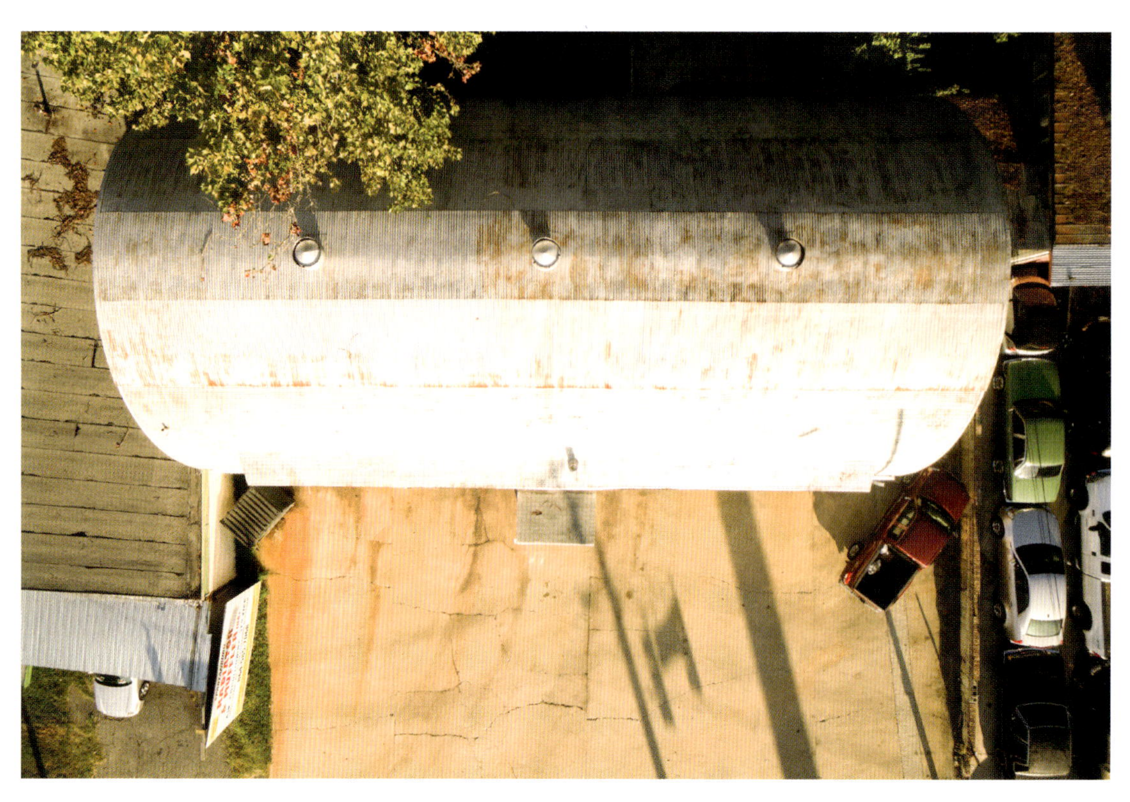

SPARTANBURG RADIATOR & MUFFLER, JOHN B WHITE SR. BLVD |

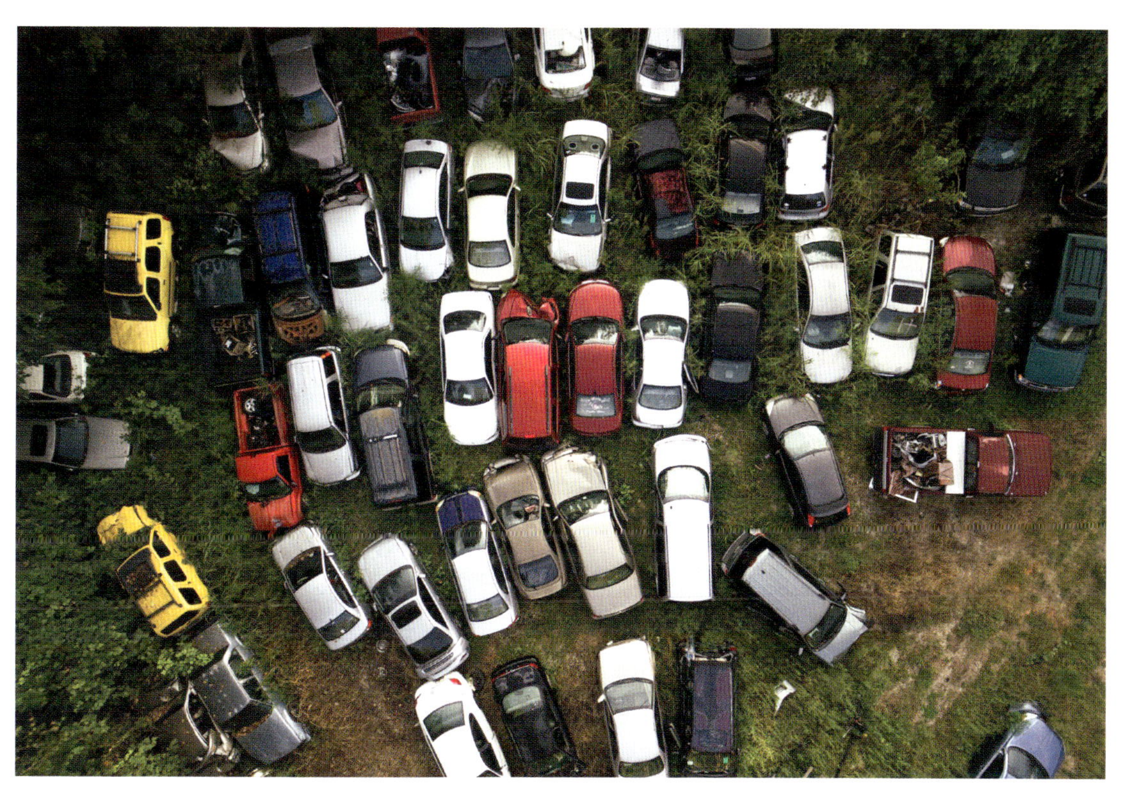

| KAND A AUTOMOTIVE

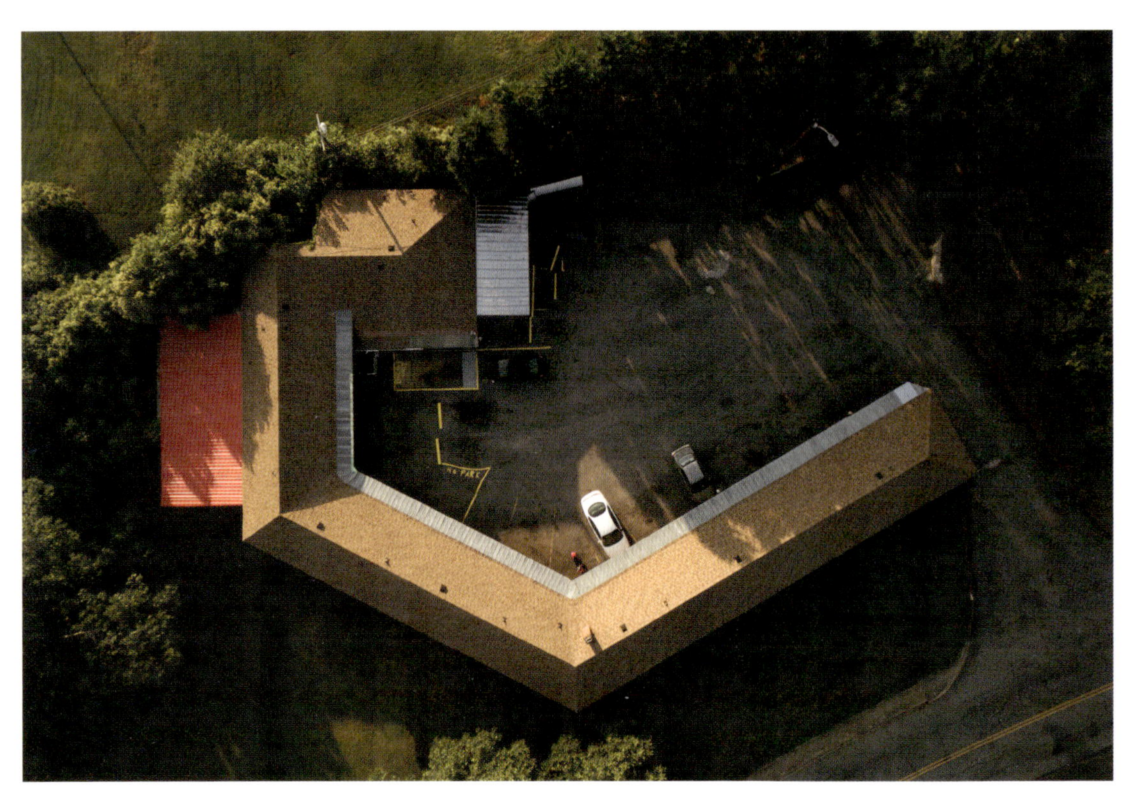

MAIN STREET MOTEL |

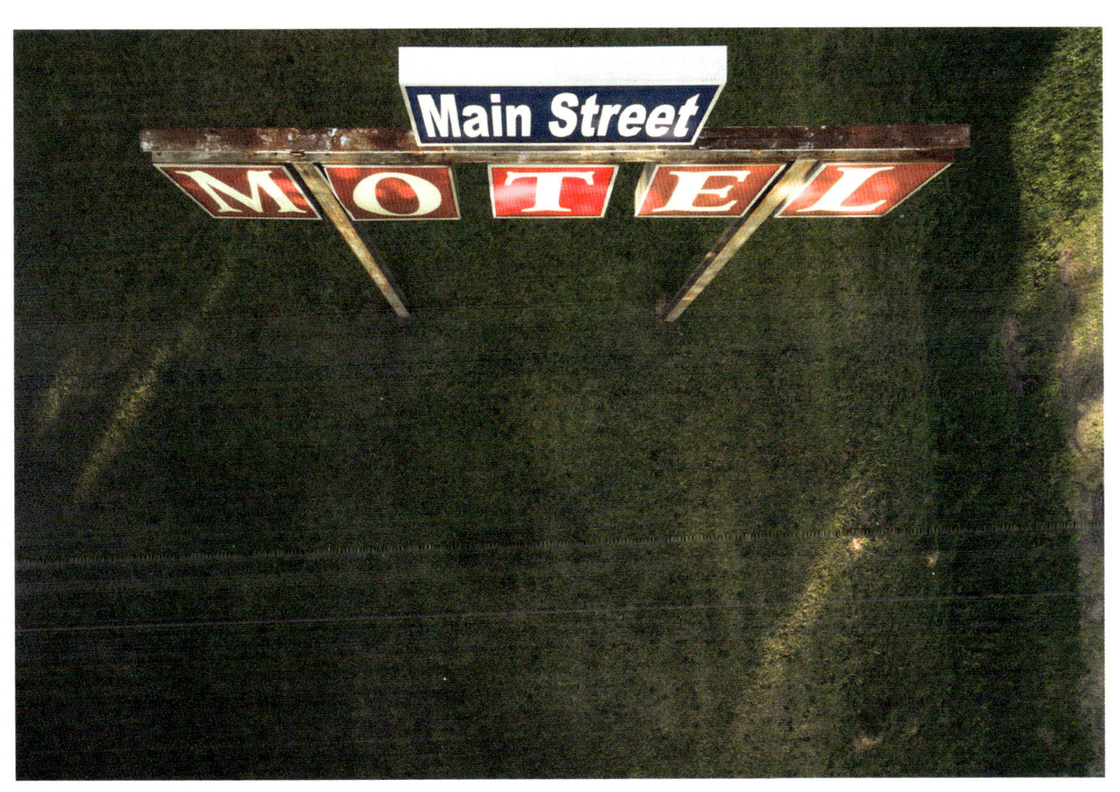

| MAIN STREET MOTEL

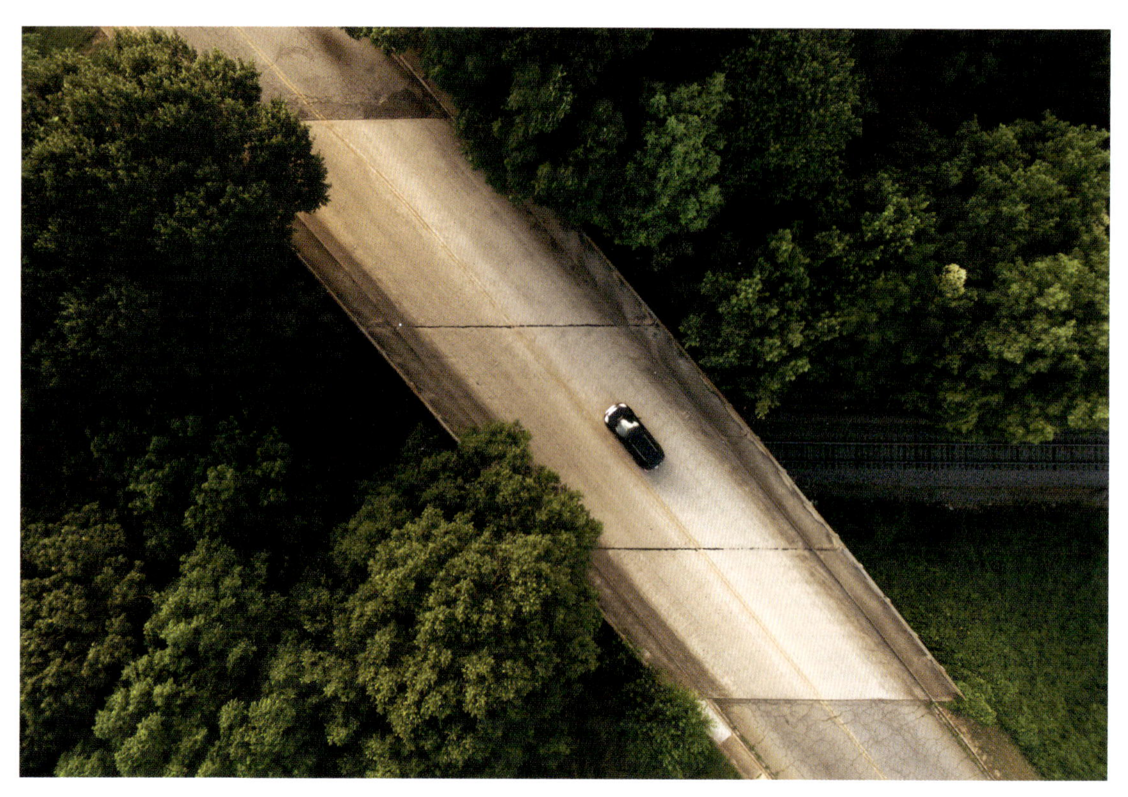

WOFFORD STREET |

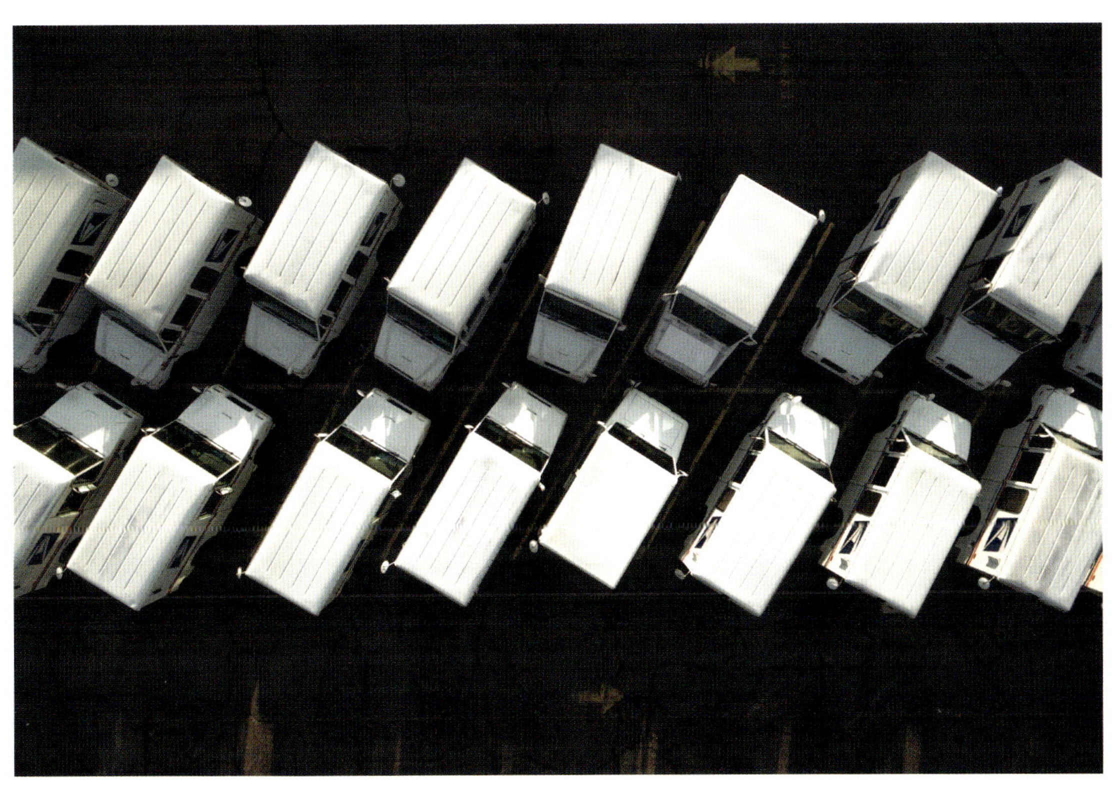

| POST OFFICE

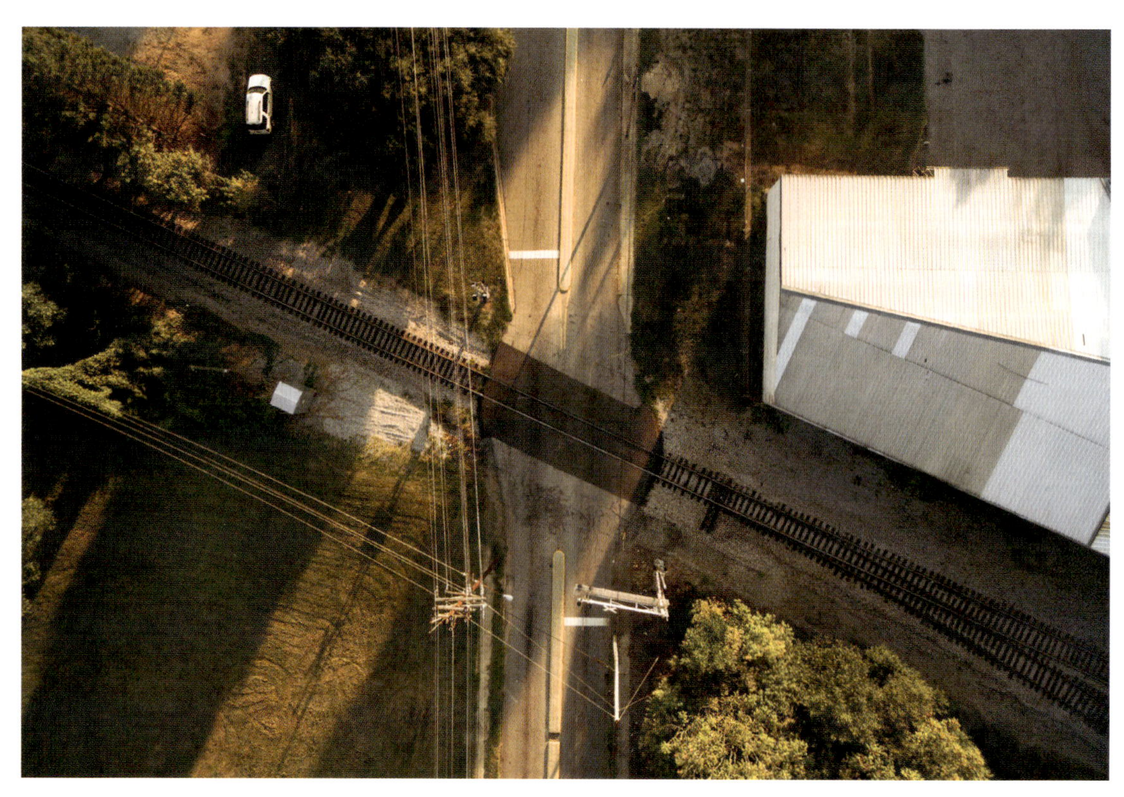

W HENRY STREET

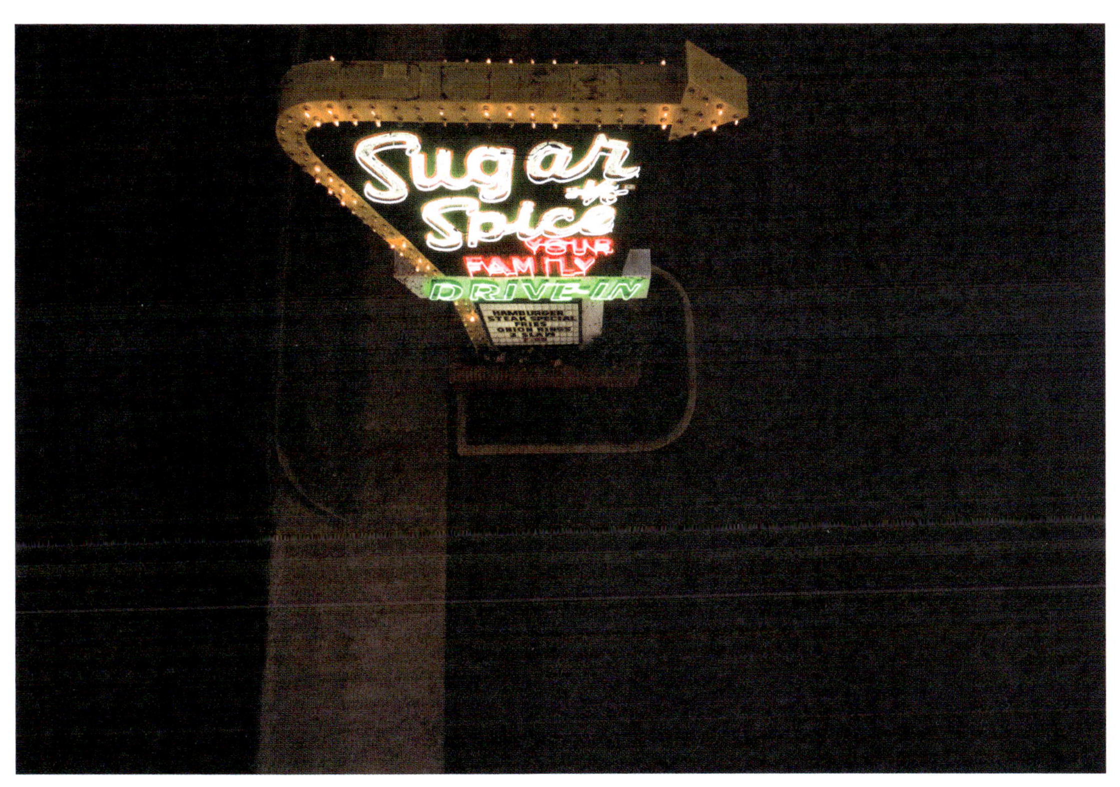

SUGAR-N-SPICE

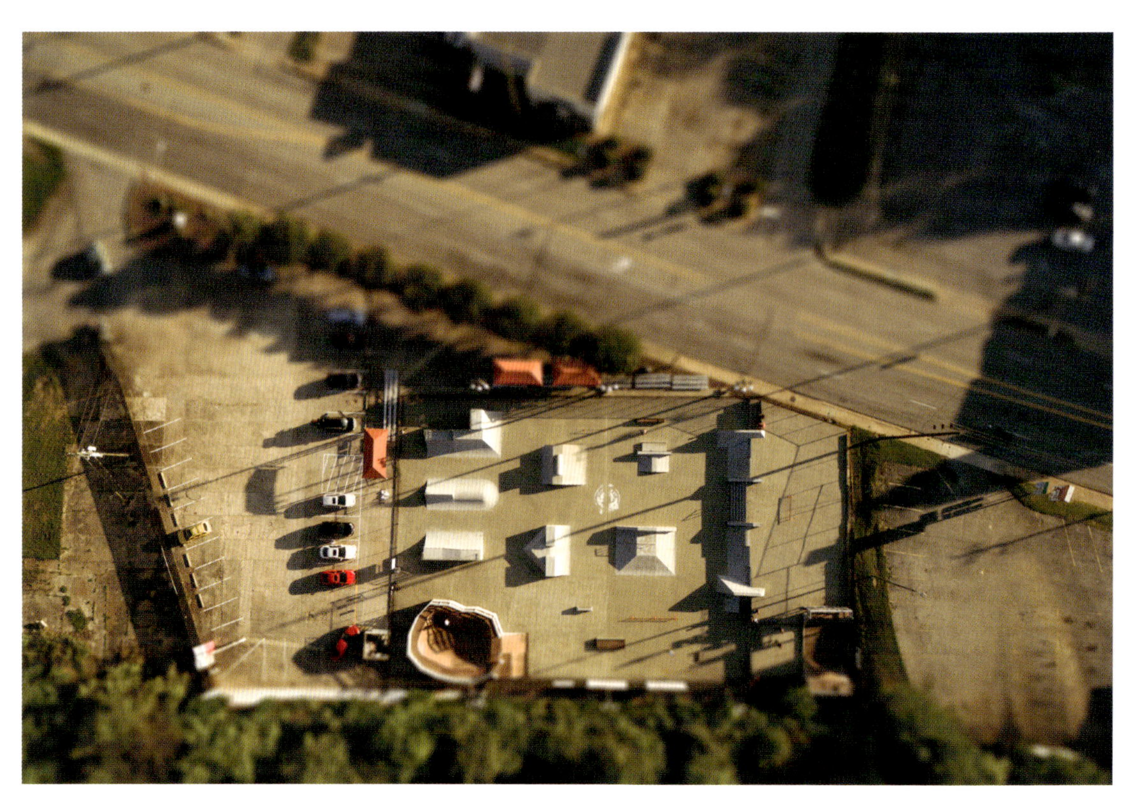

HOT SPOT SKATE PARK, EVENING |

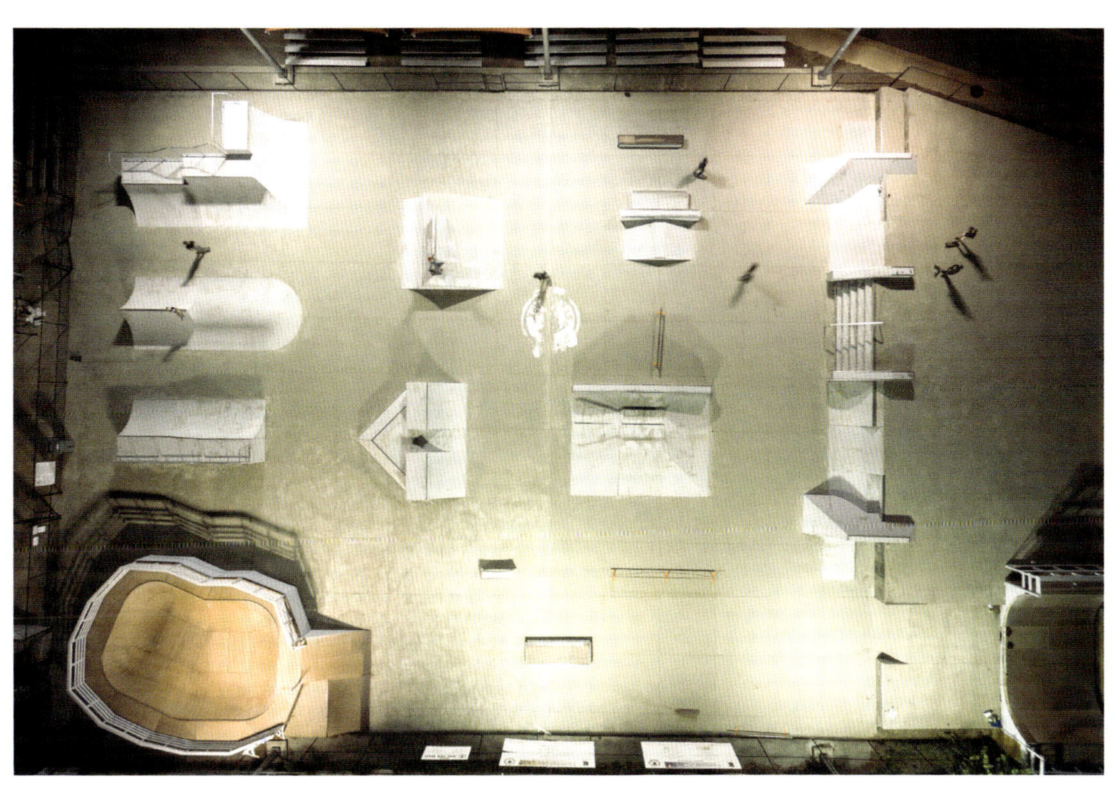

| HOT SPOT SKATE PARK, NIGHT

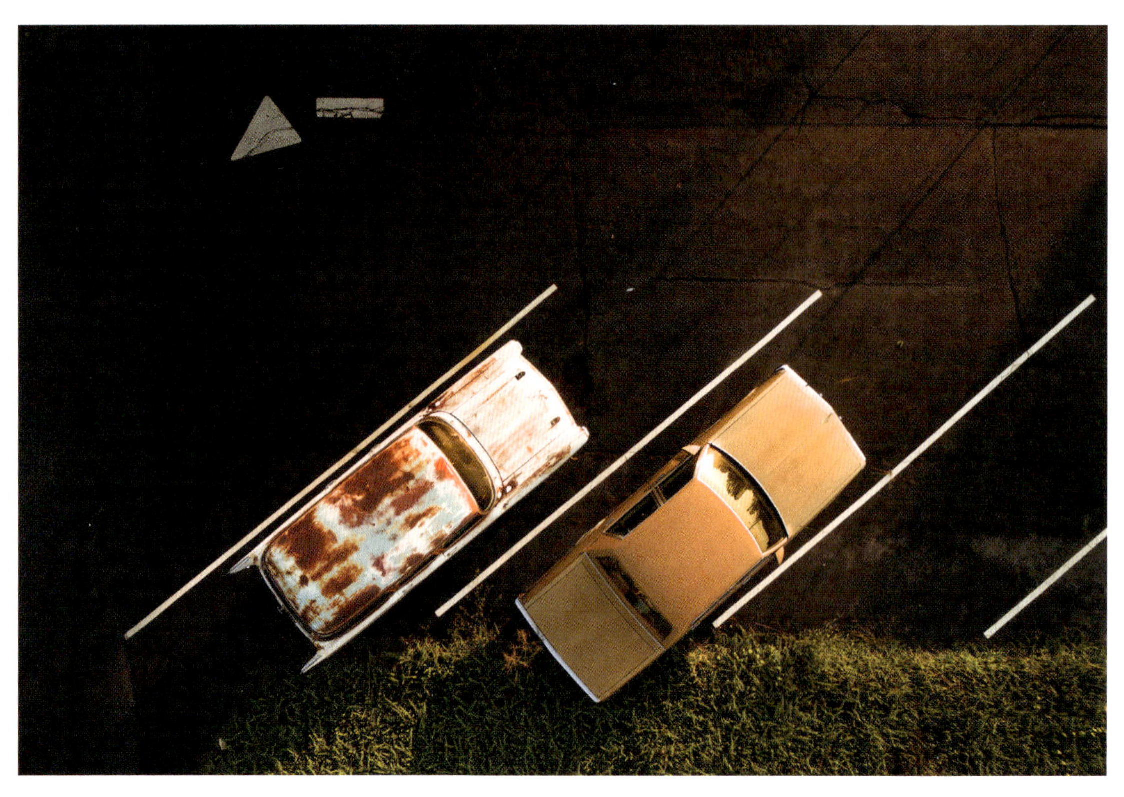

HARRIS AUTOMOTIVE |

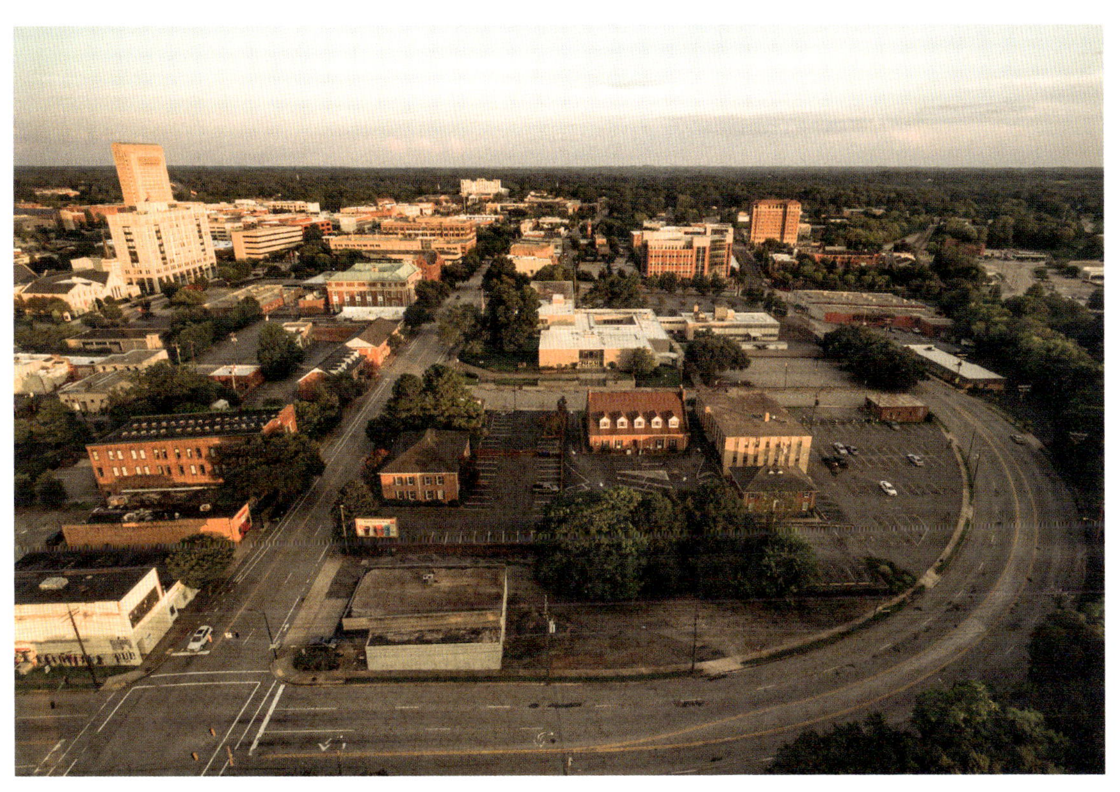

S DANIEL MORGAN AVENUE

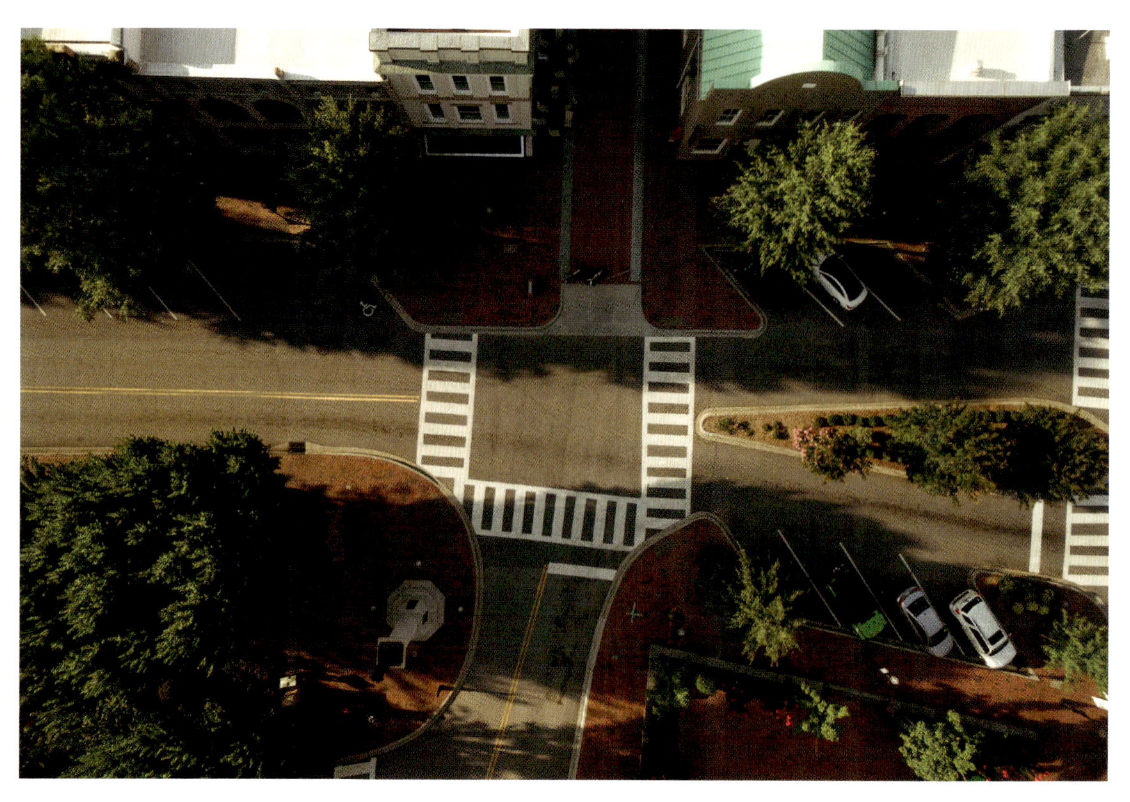

MAIN AND MAGNOLIA |

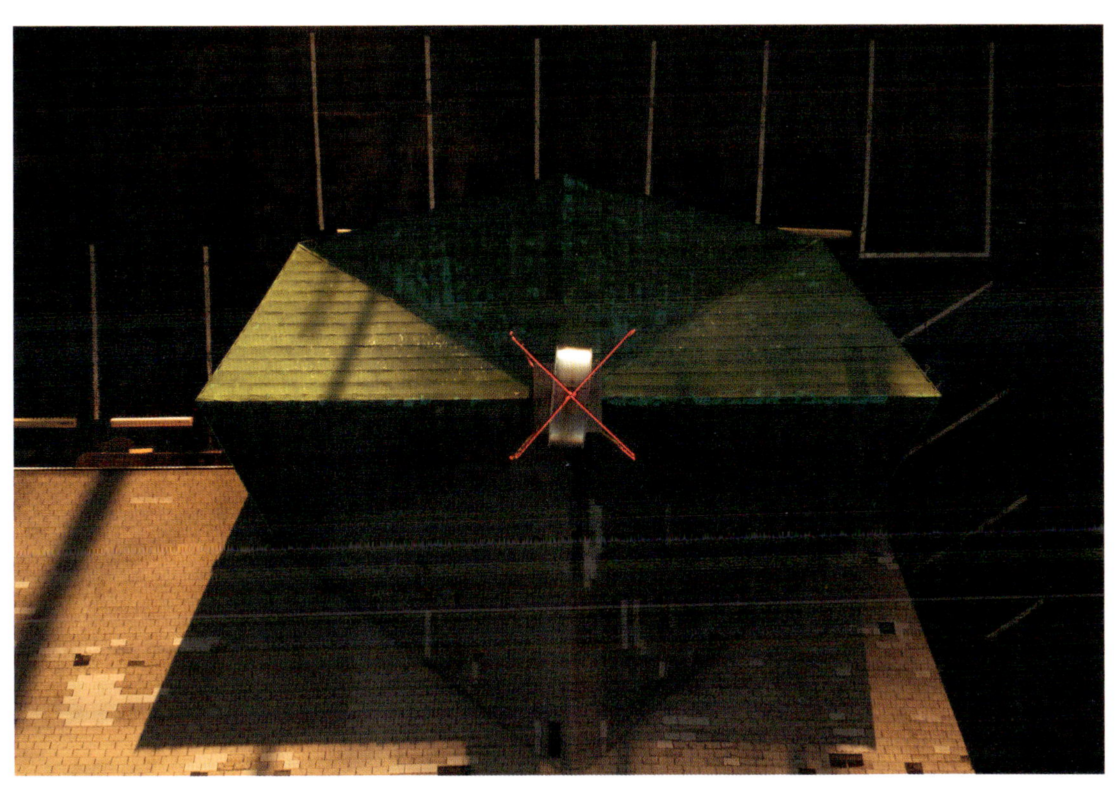

KRISPY KREME

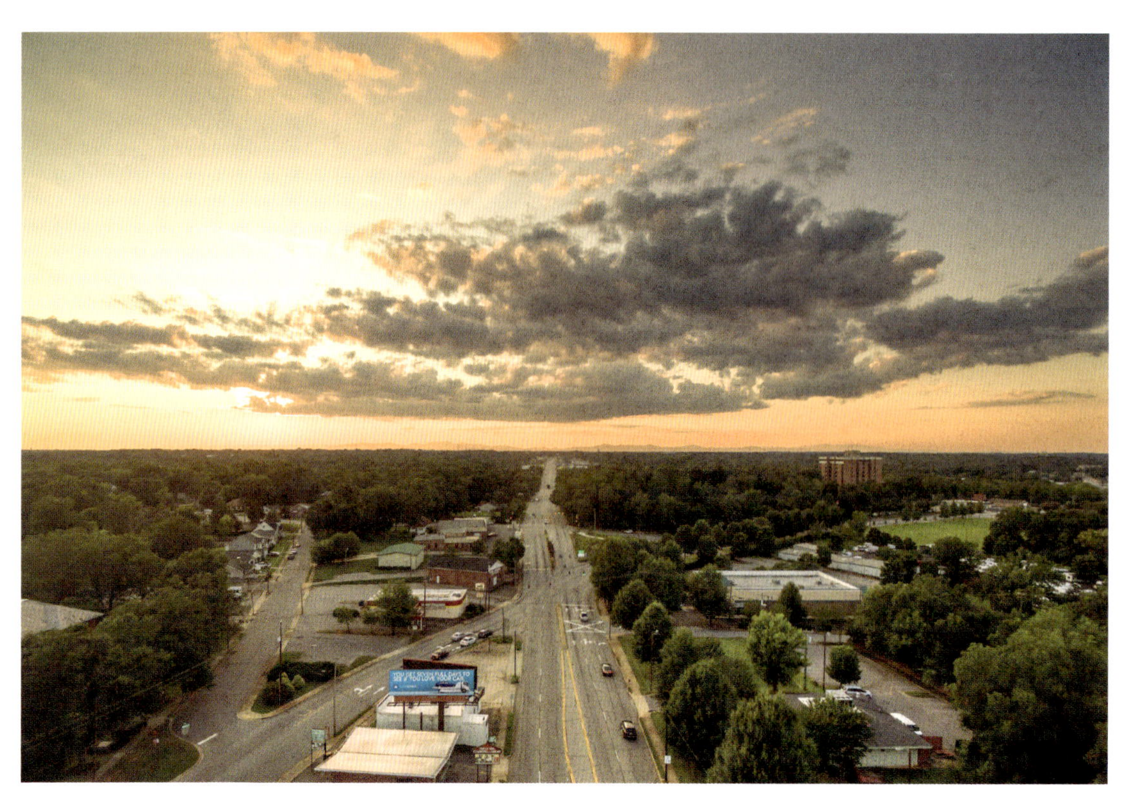

N CHURCH STREET

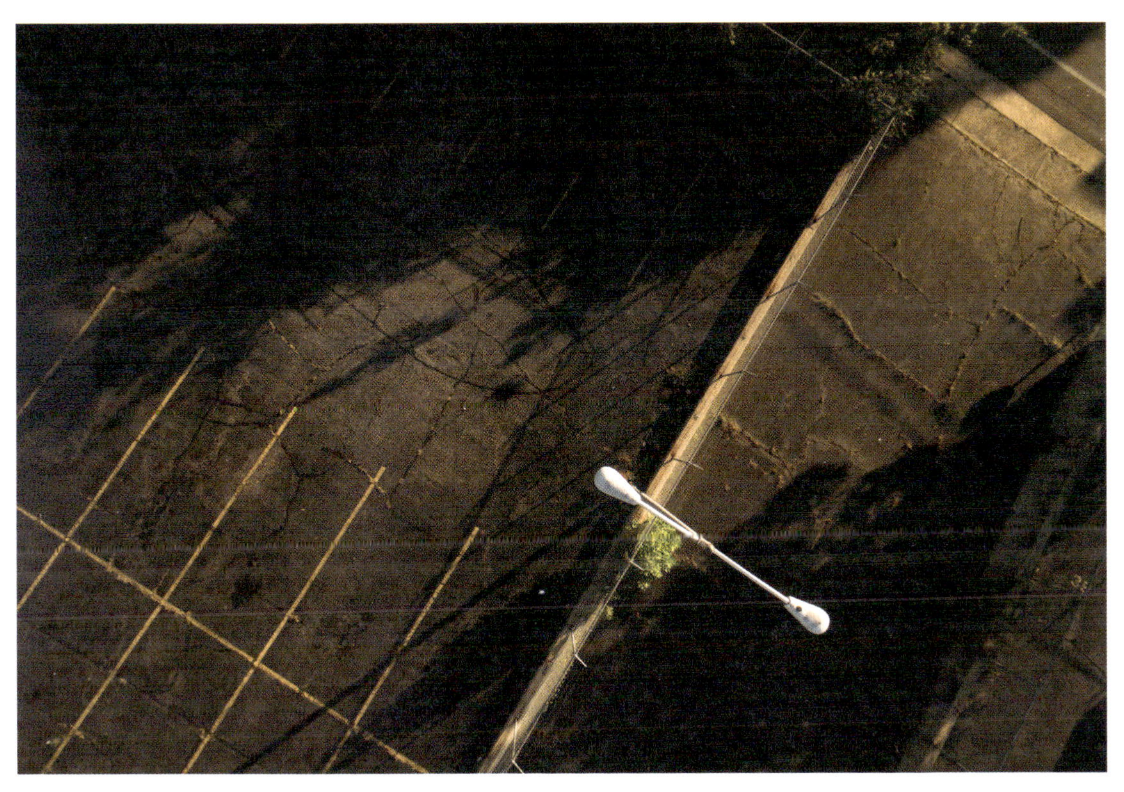

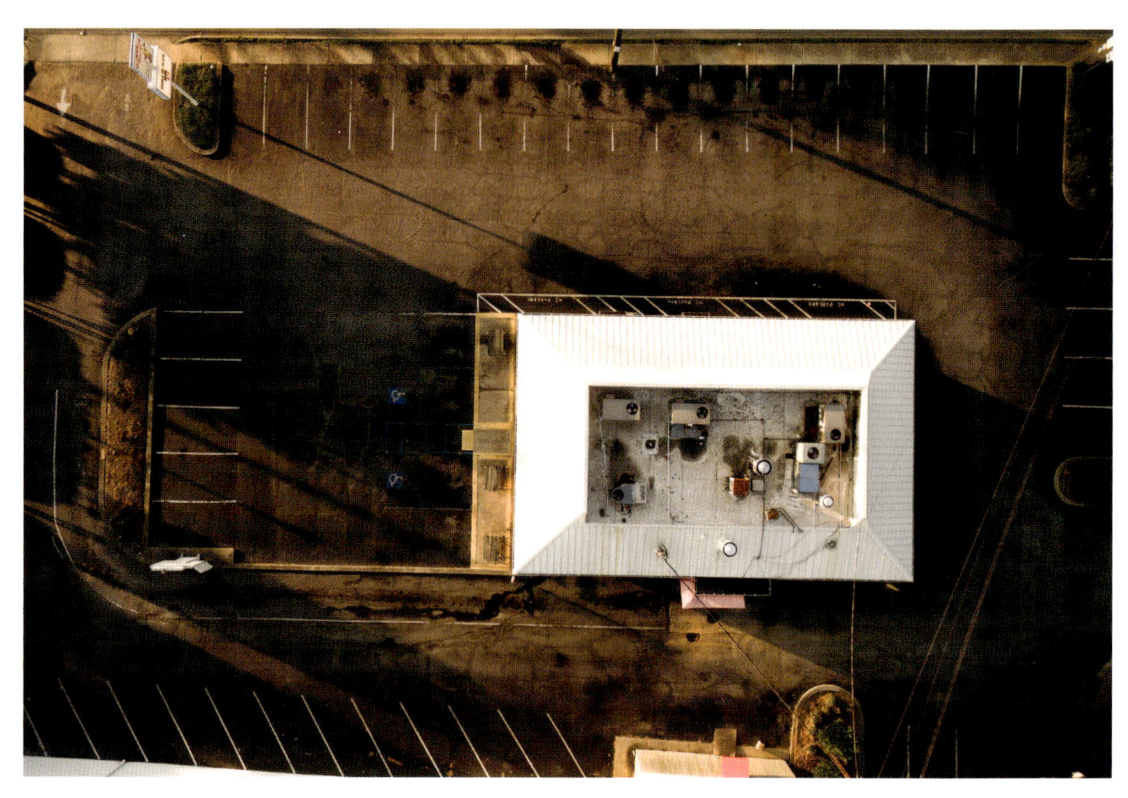

BOOTS' & SONNY'S, MORNING |

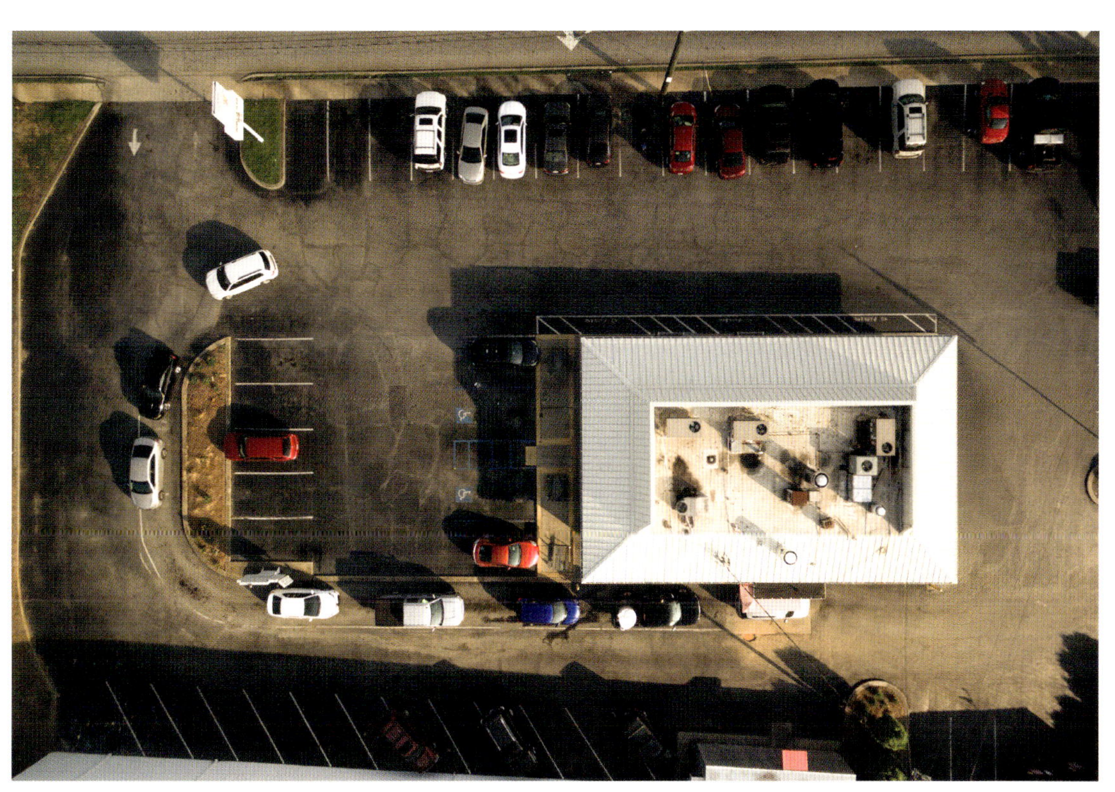

BOOTS' & SONNY'S, EVENING

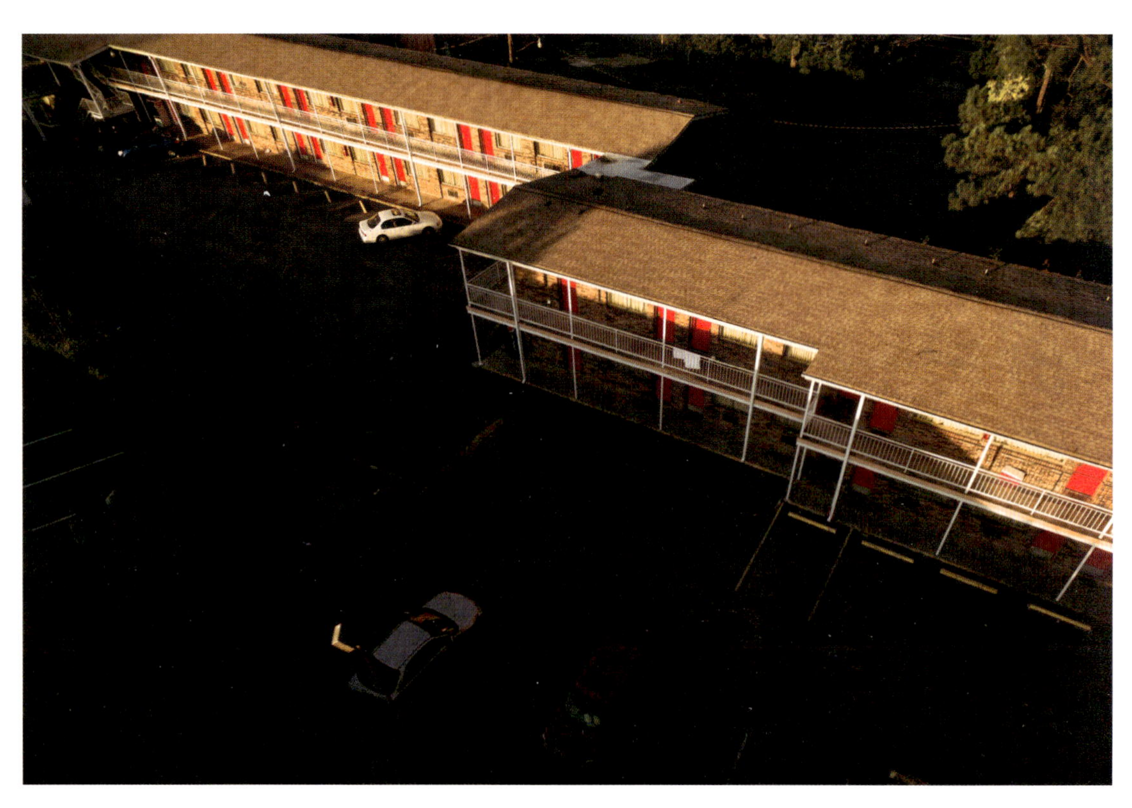

SUPER LODGE, E MAIN STREET |

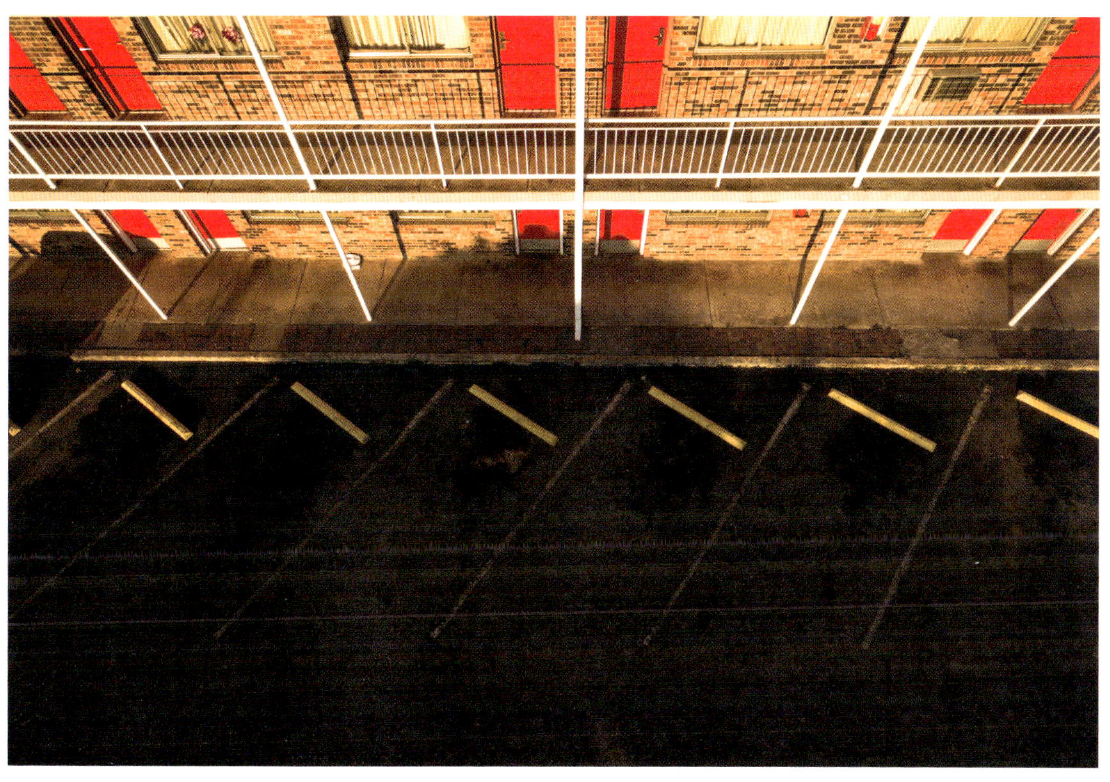

RED DOORS

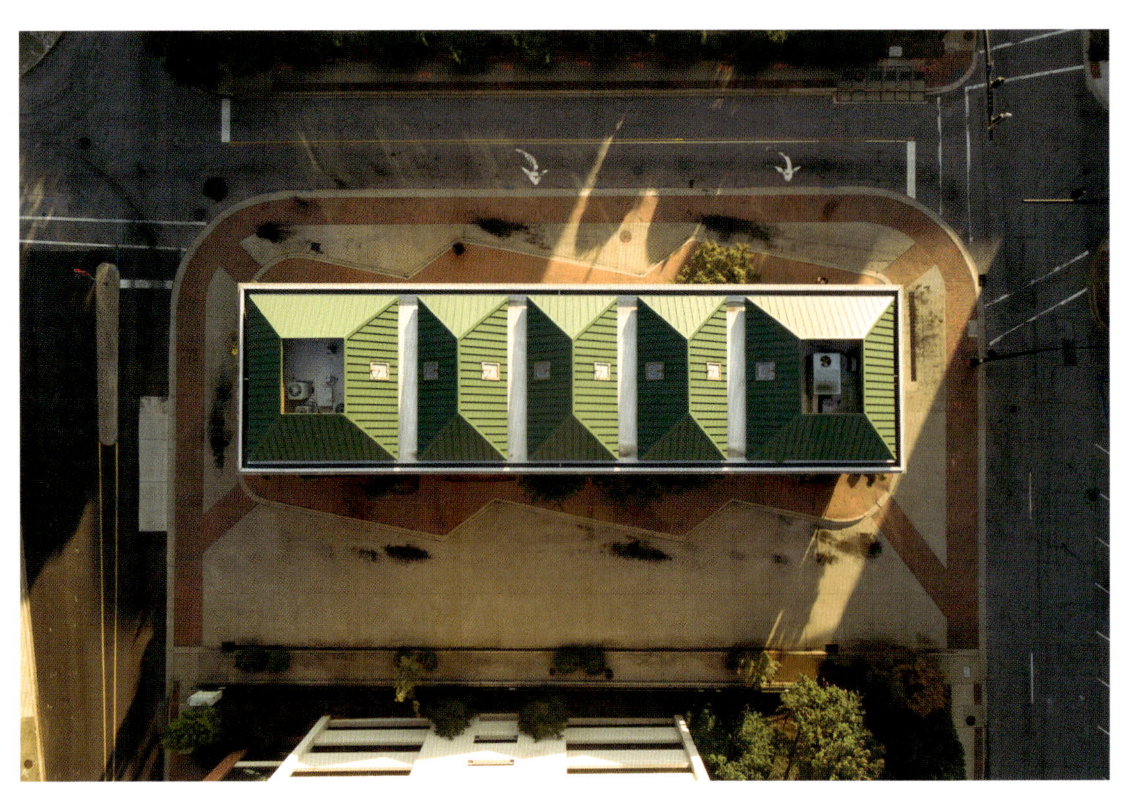

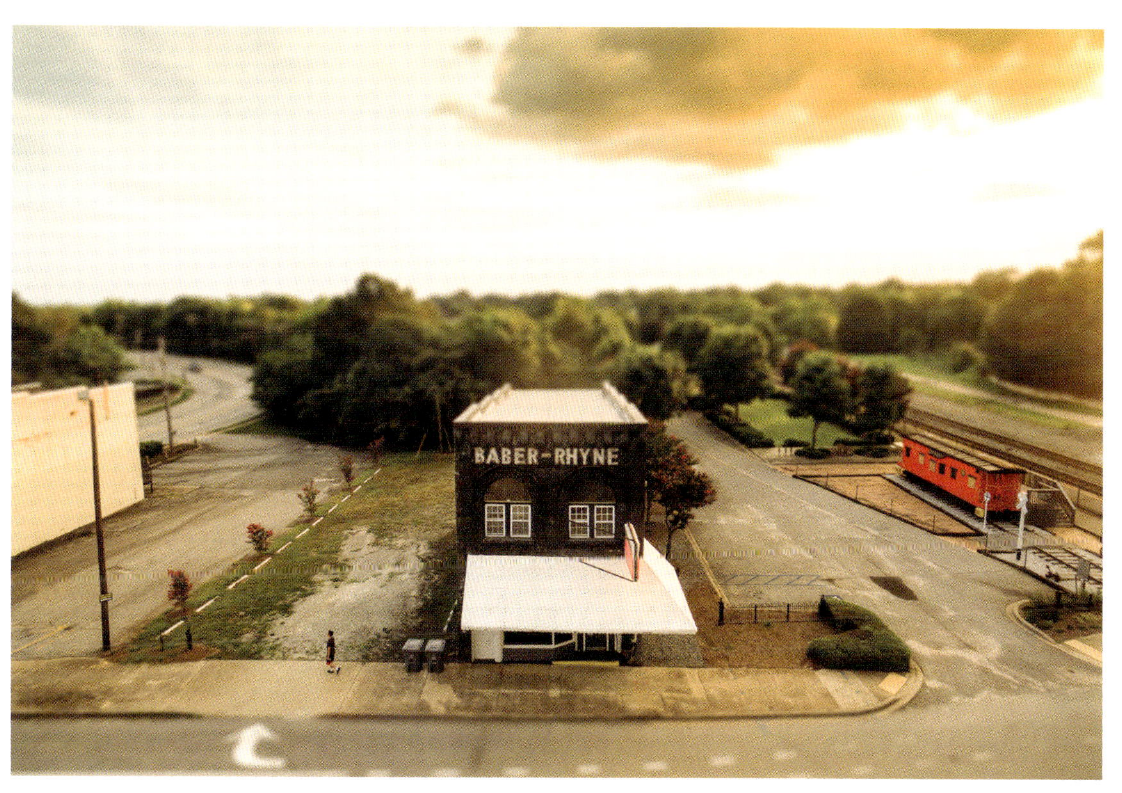

BABER-RHYNE BUILDING

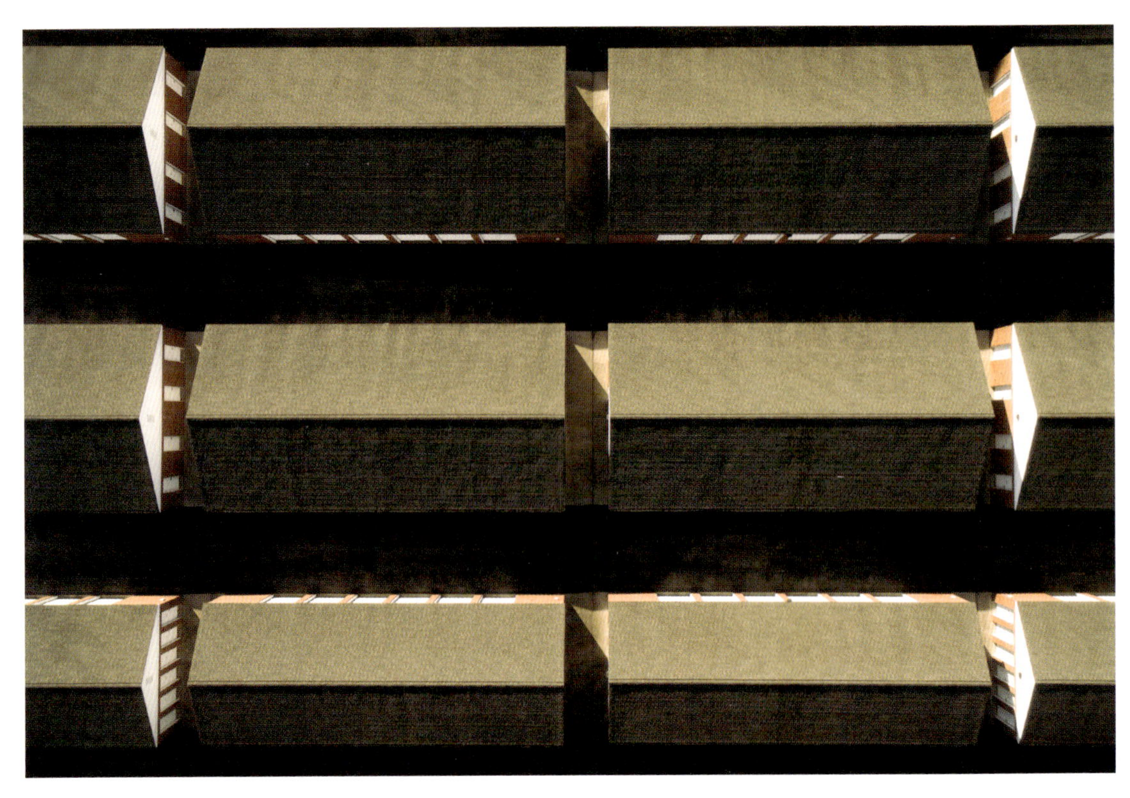

U-STOR, PINE STREET |

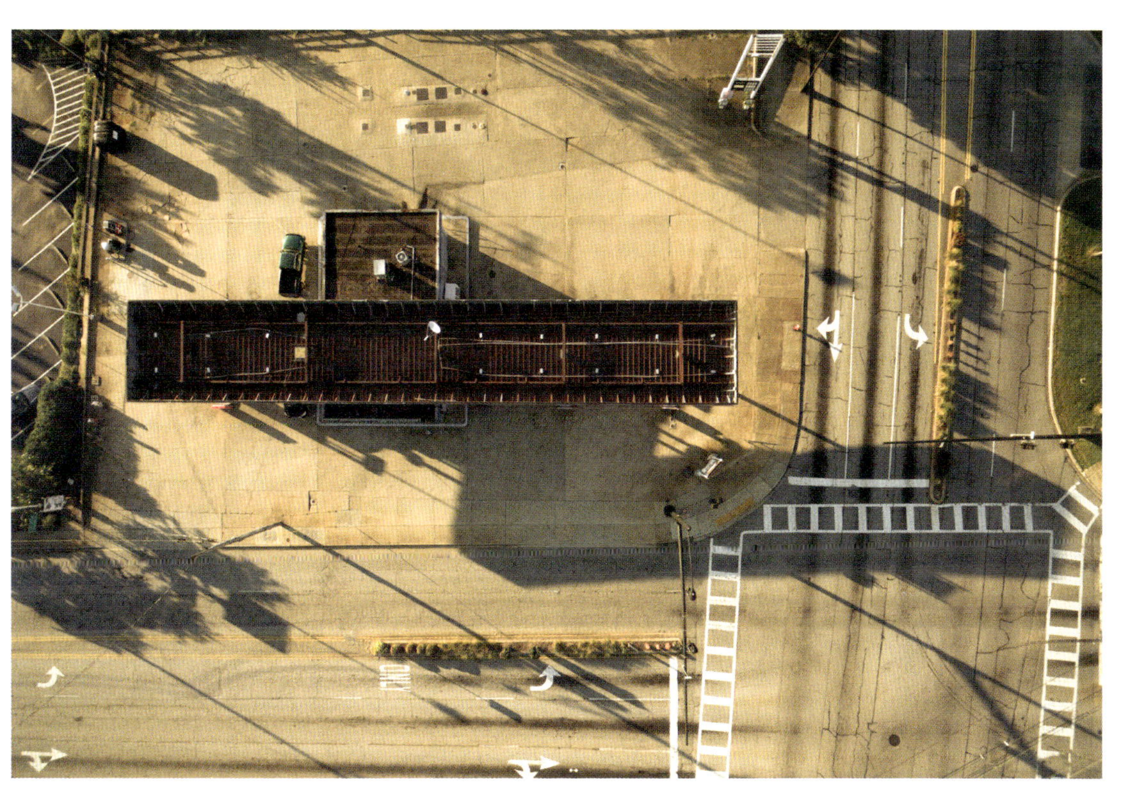

SOUTHERN CONVENIENCE STORES, W HENRY STREET

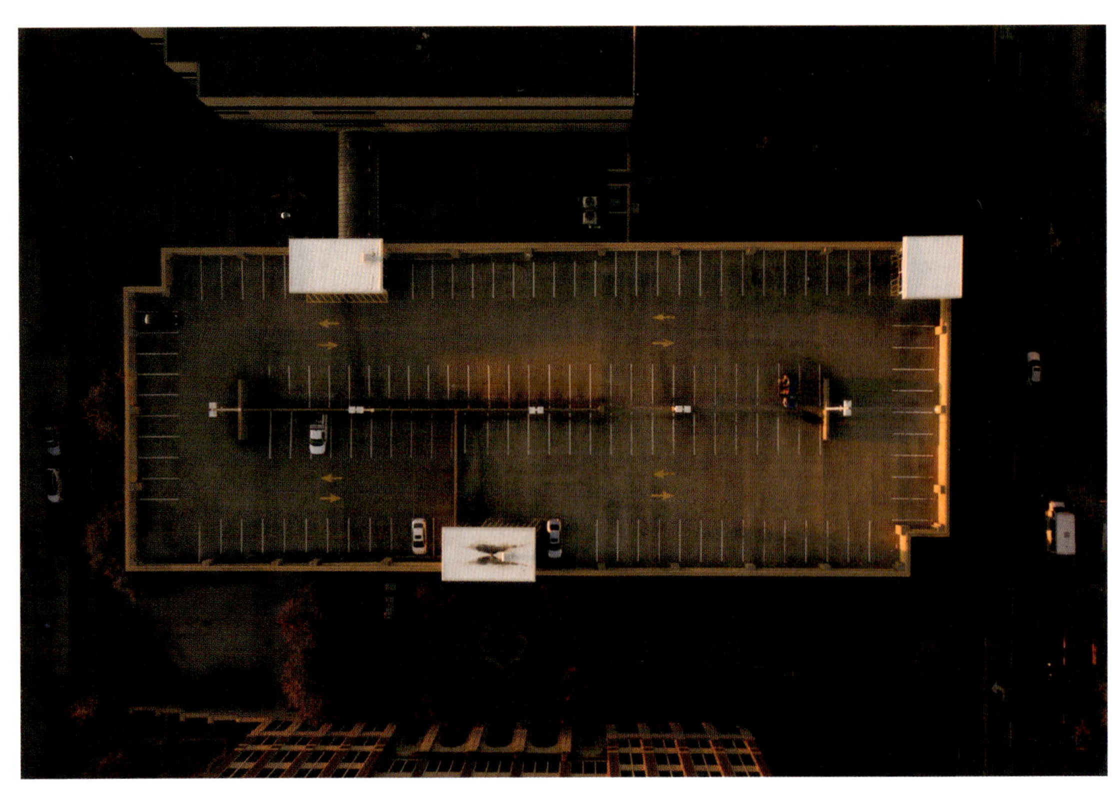

MAGNOLIA AND CHURCH STREET PARKING DECK |

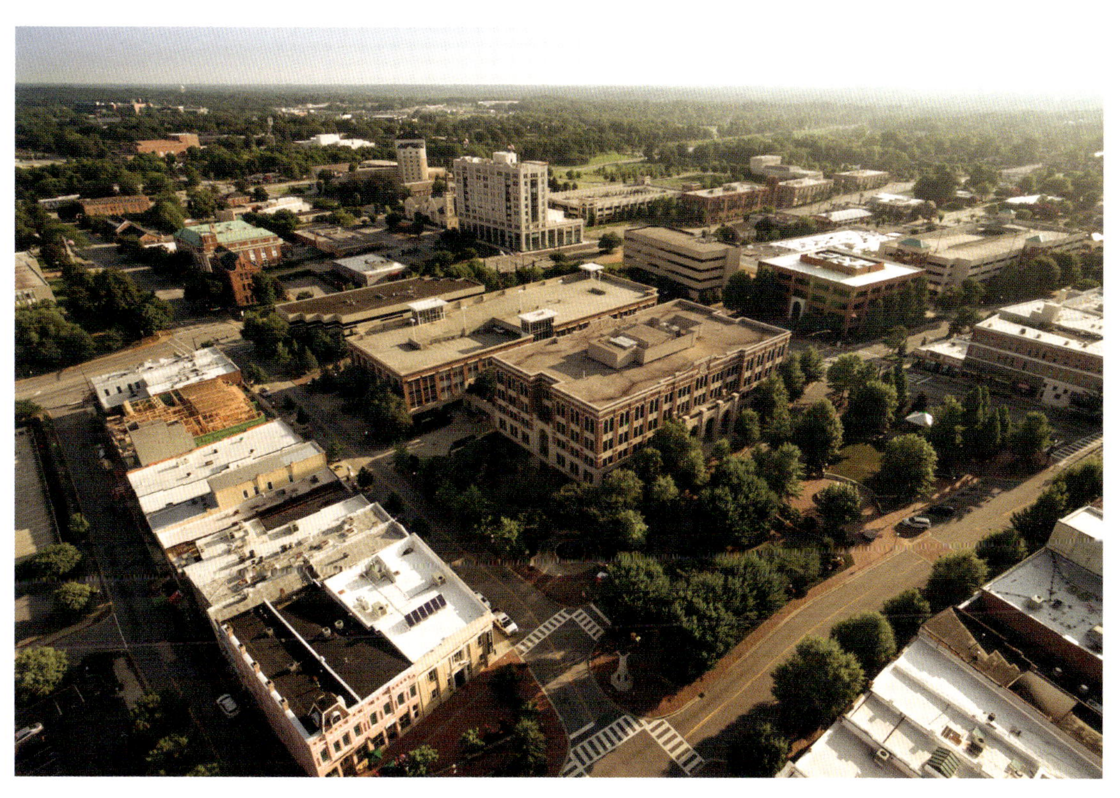

MORGAN SQUARE

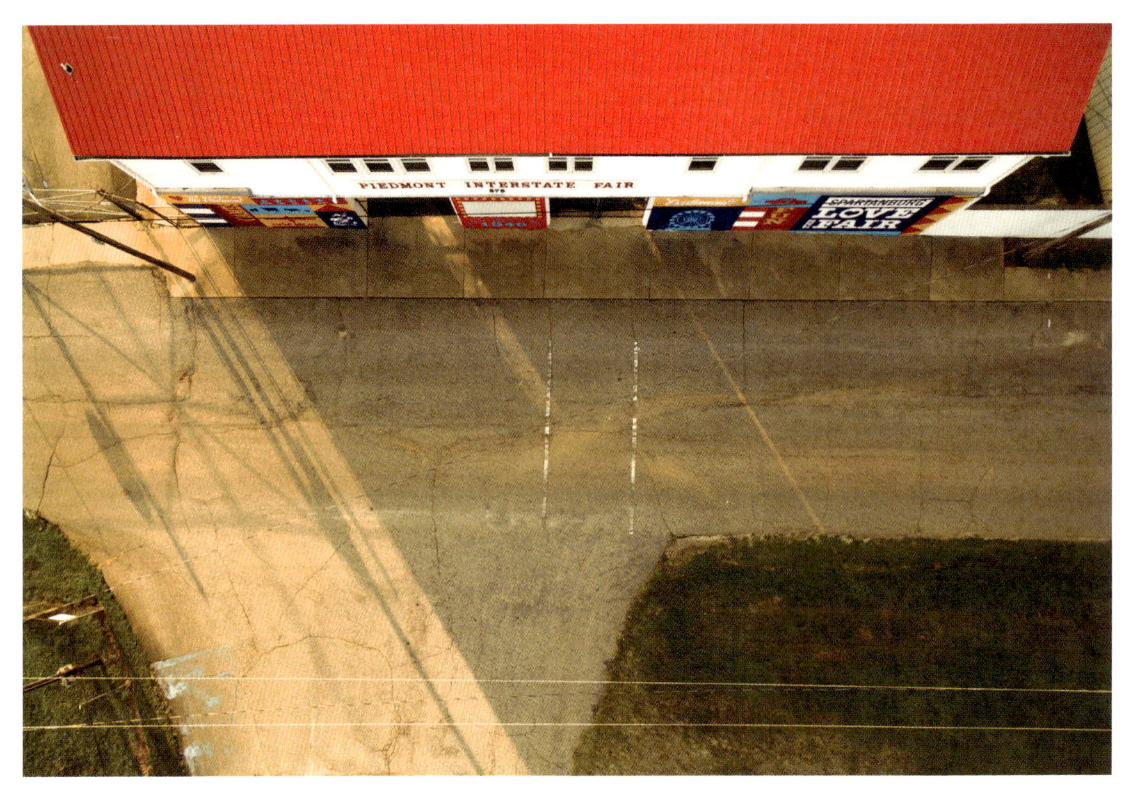

PIEDMONT INTERSTATE FAIR |

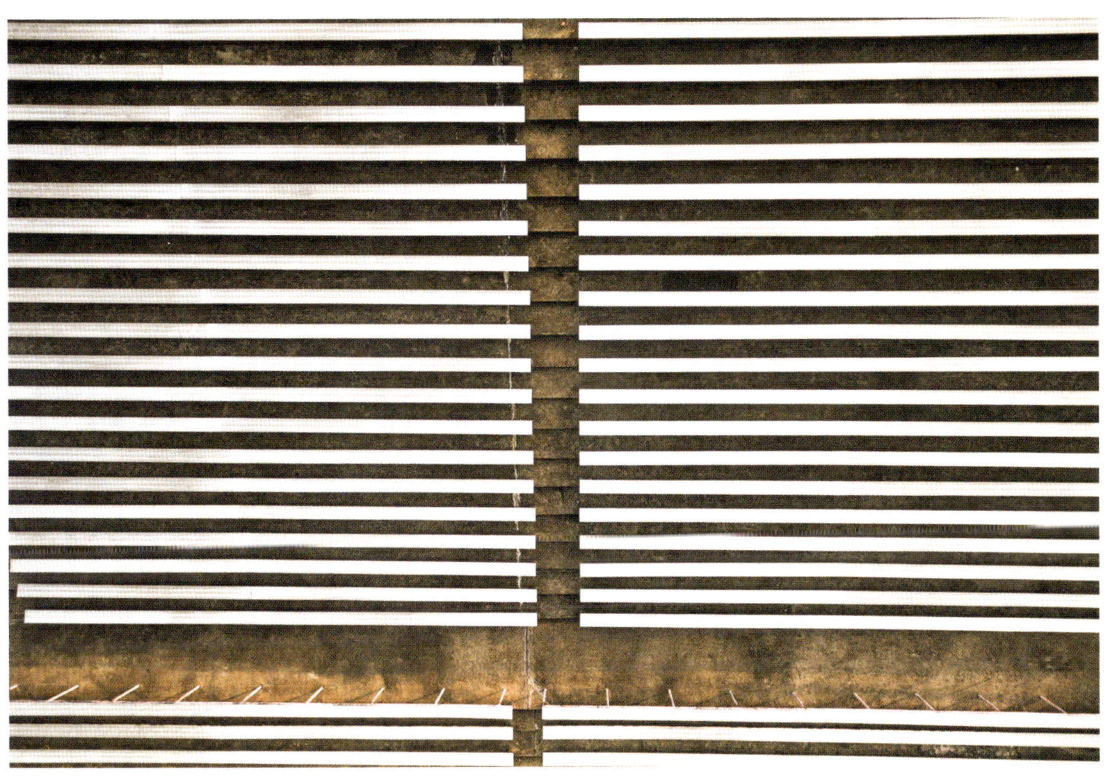

| FAIRGROUND BLEACHERS

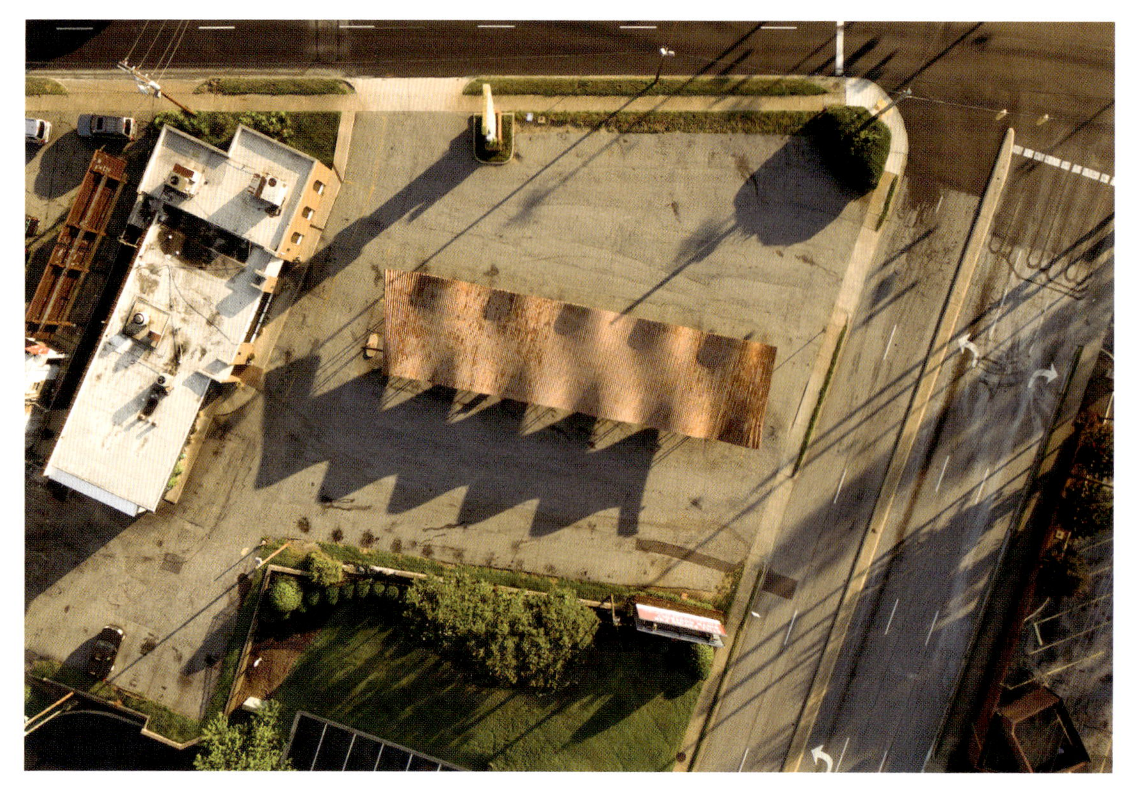

SUGAR-N-SPICE |

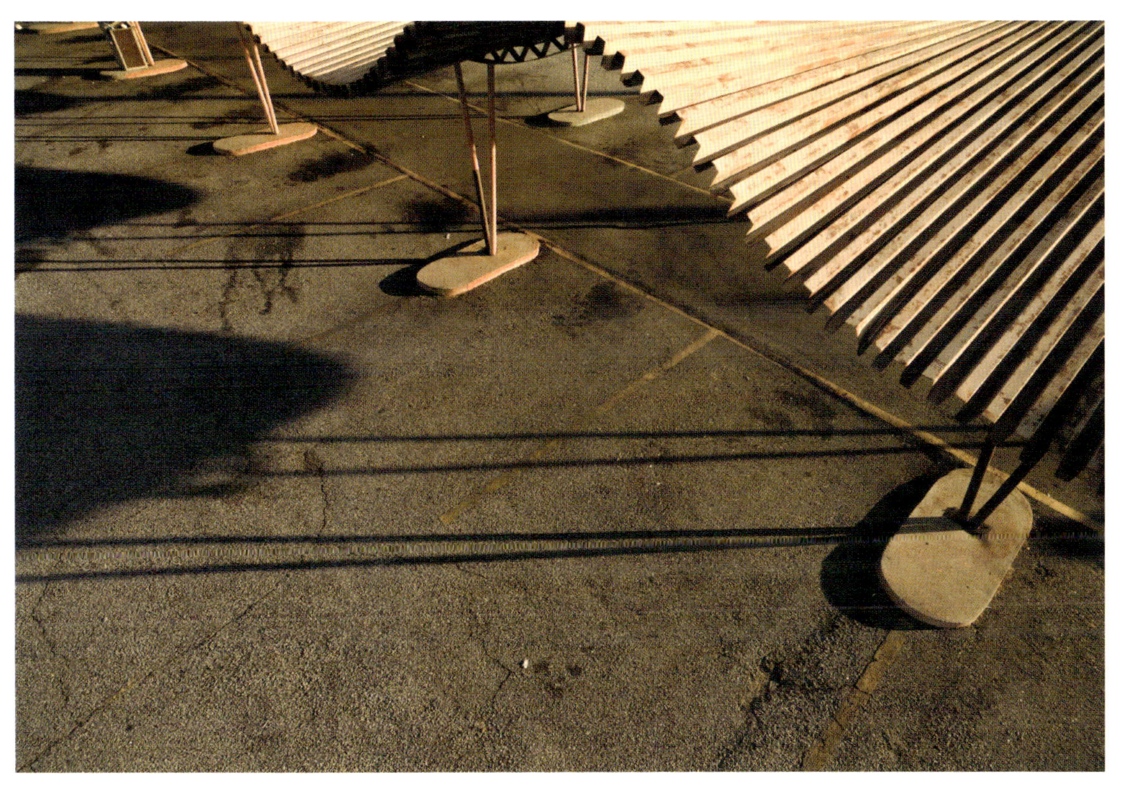

SUGAR-N-SPICE

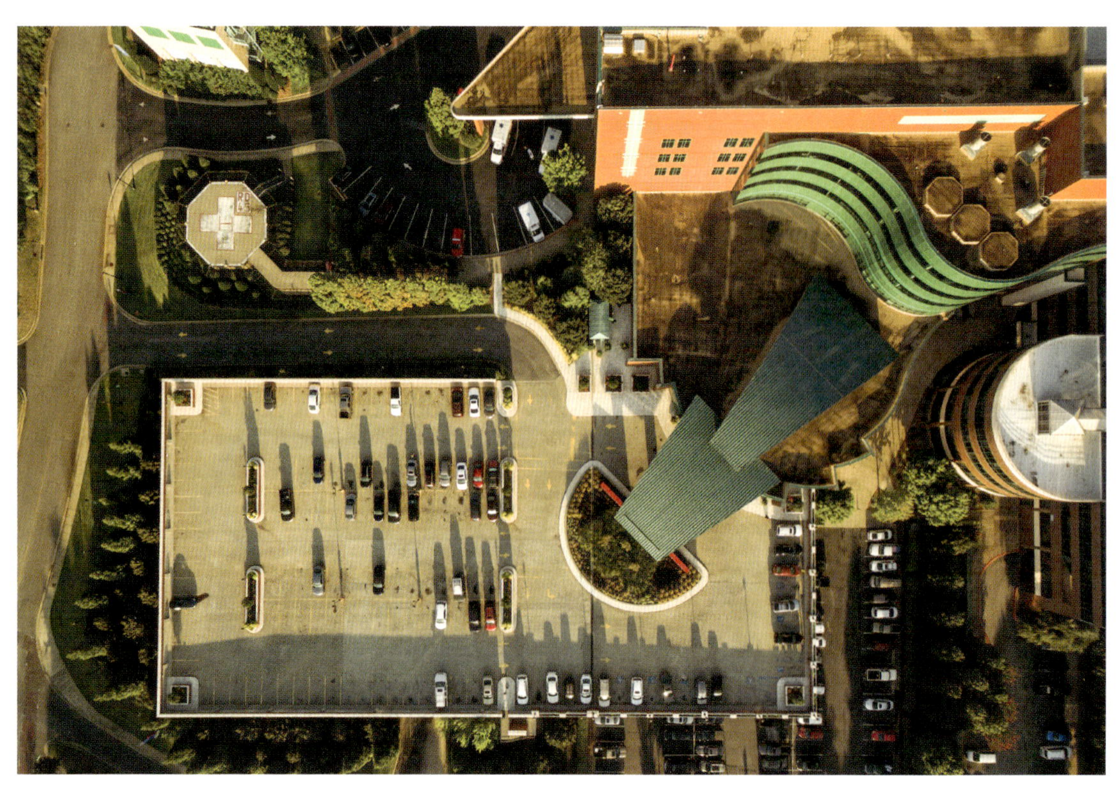

SPARTANBURG REGIONAL |

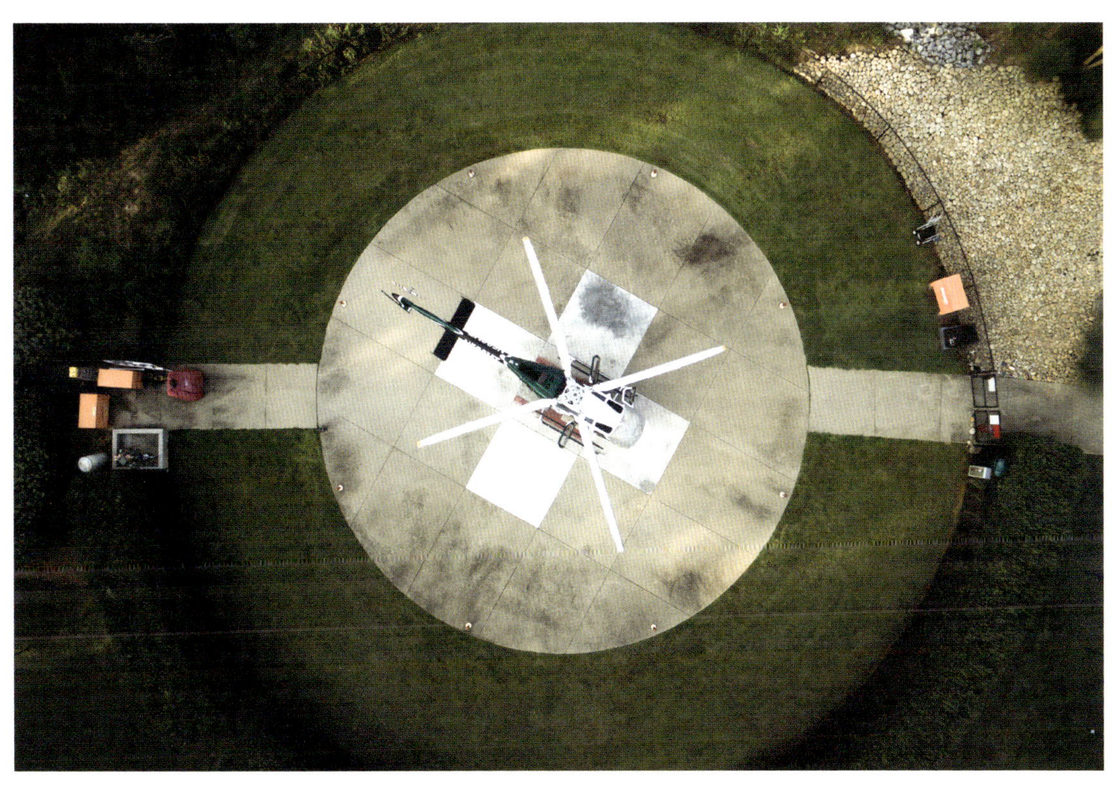

HELI PAD

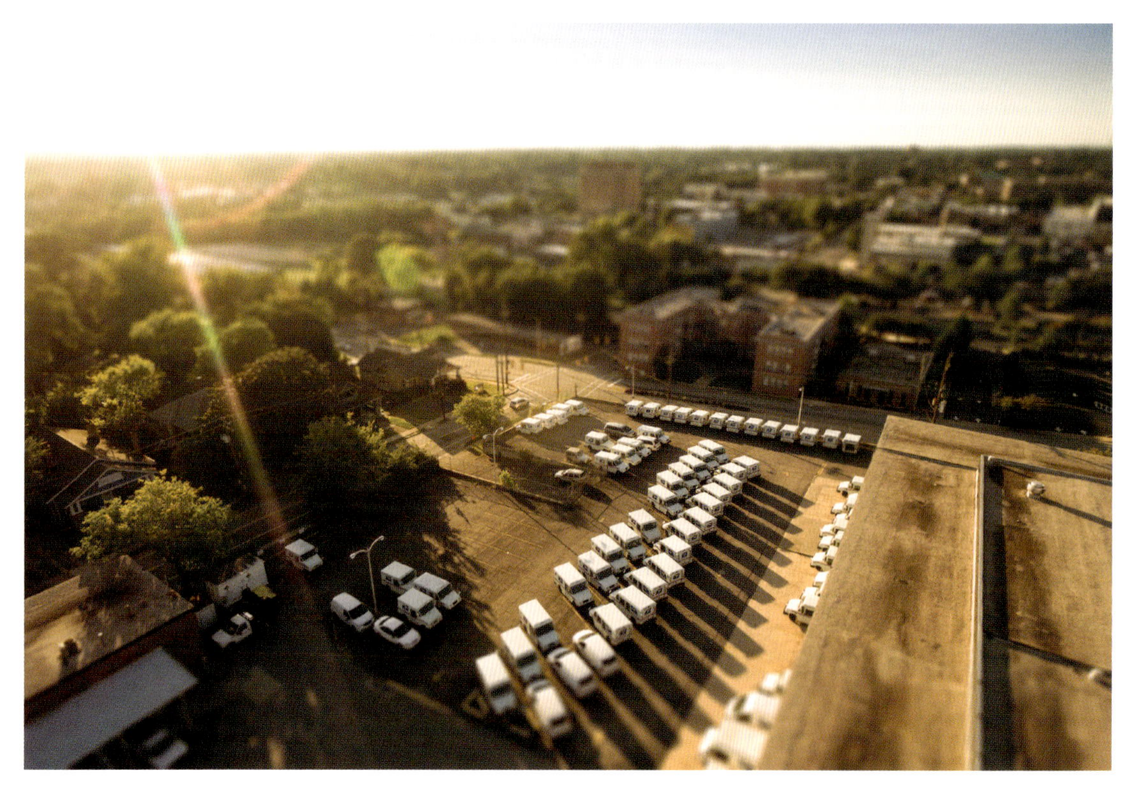

POST OFFICE |

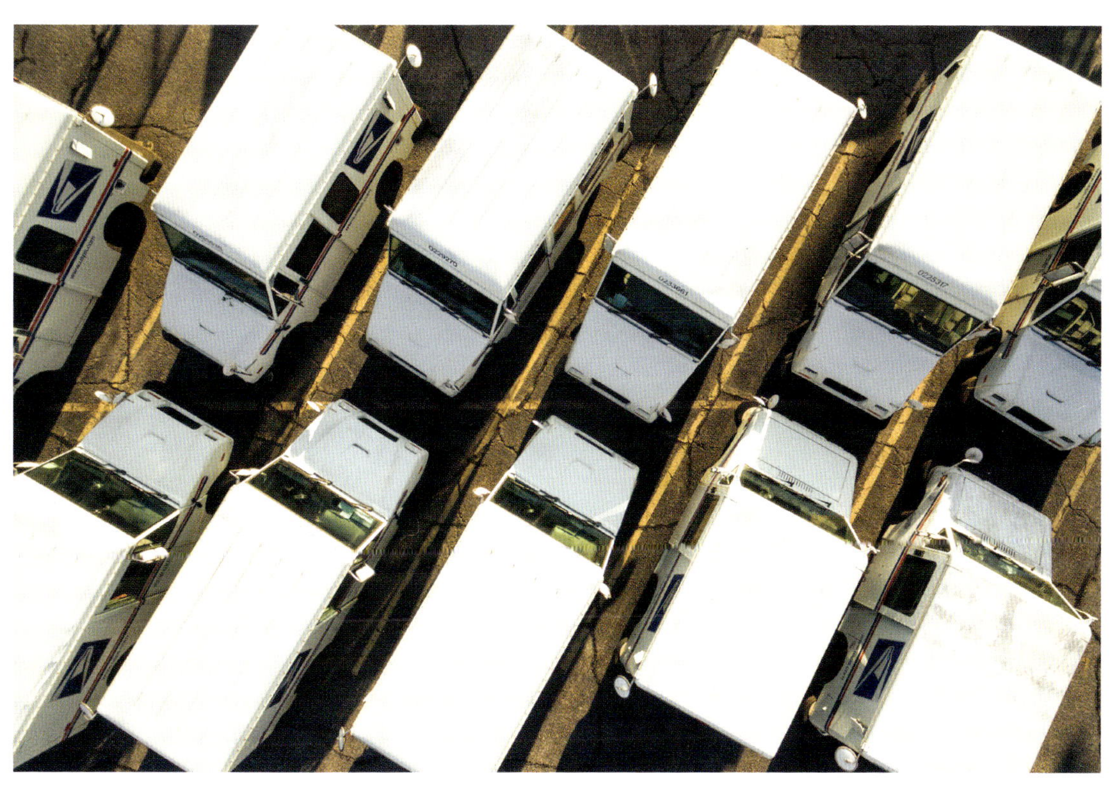

RETURN TO SENDER

71

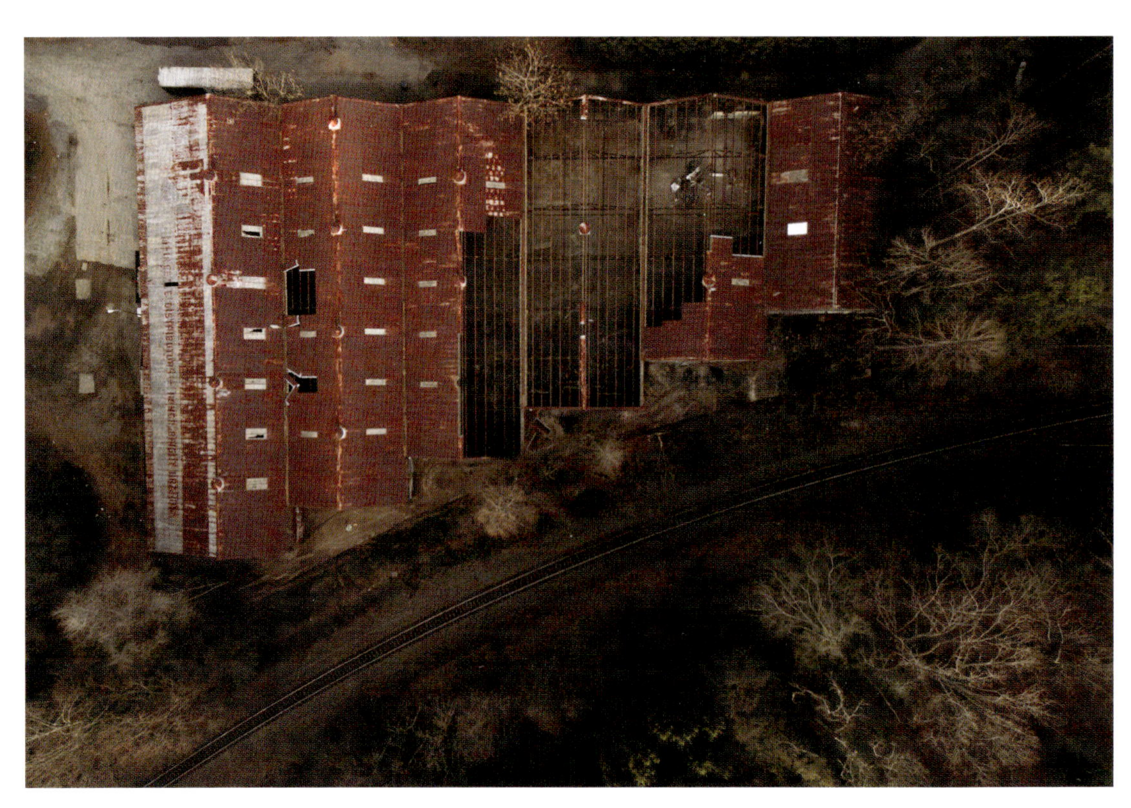

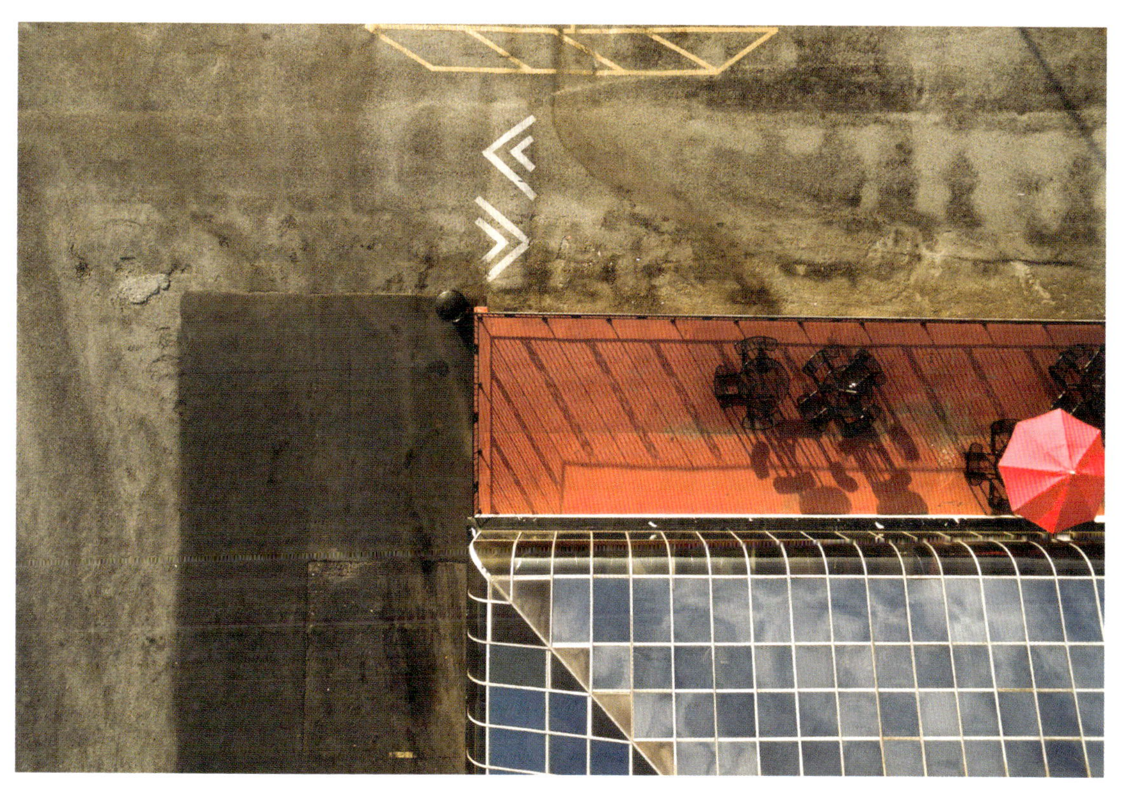

| THE BEACON

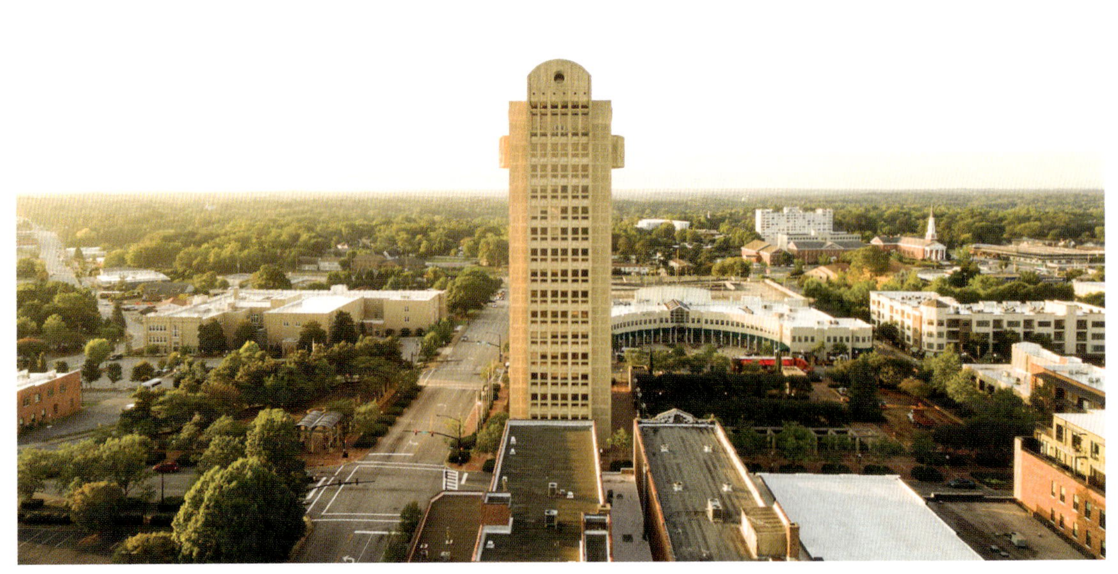

DENNY'S BUILDING, MORNING |

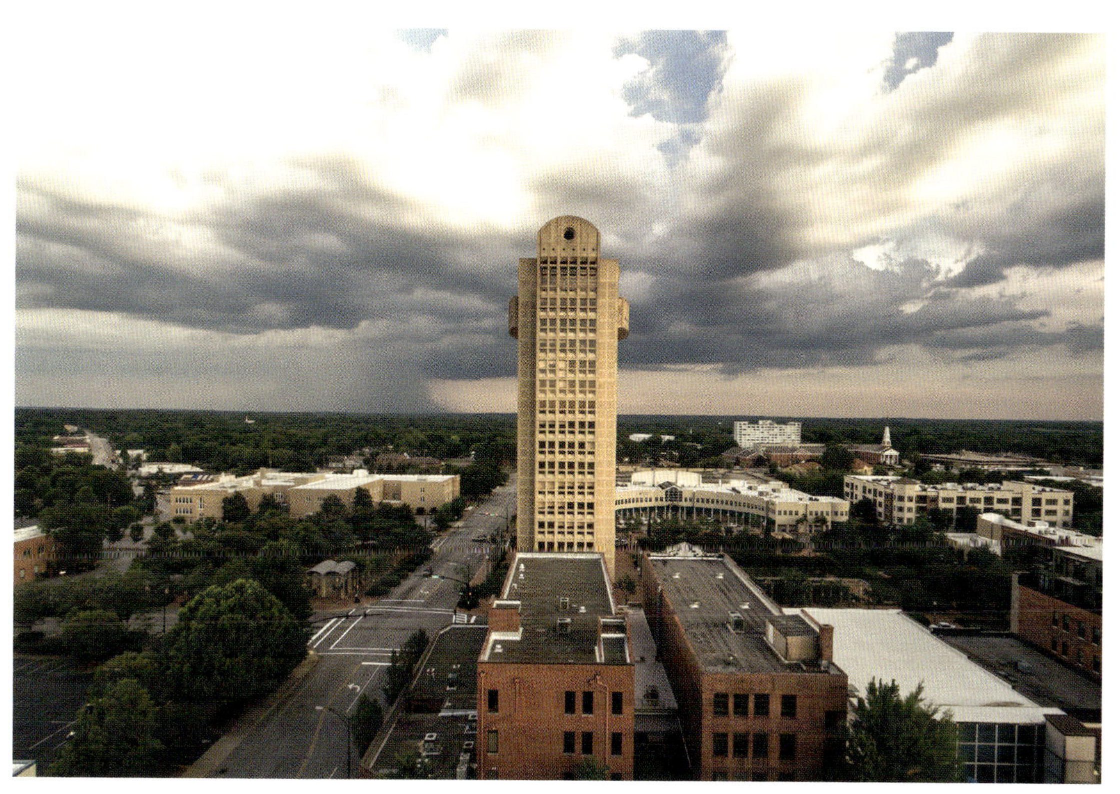

DENNY'S BUILDING, EVENING

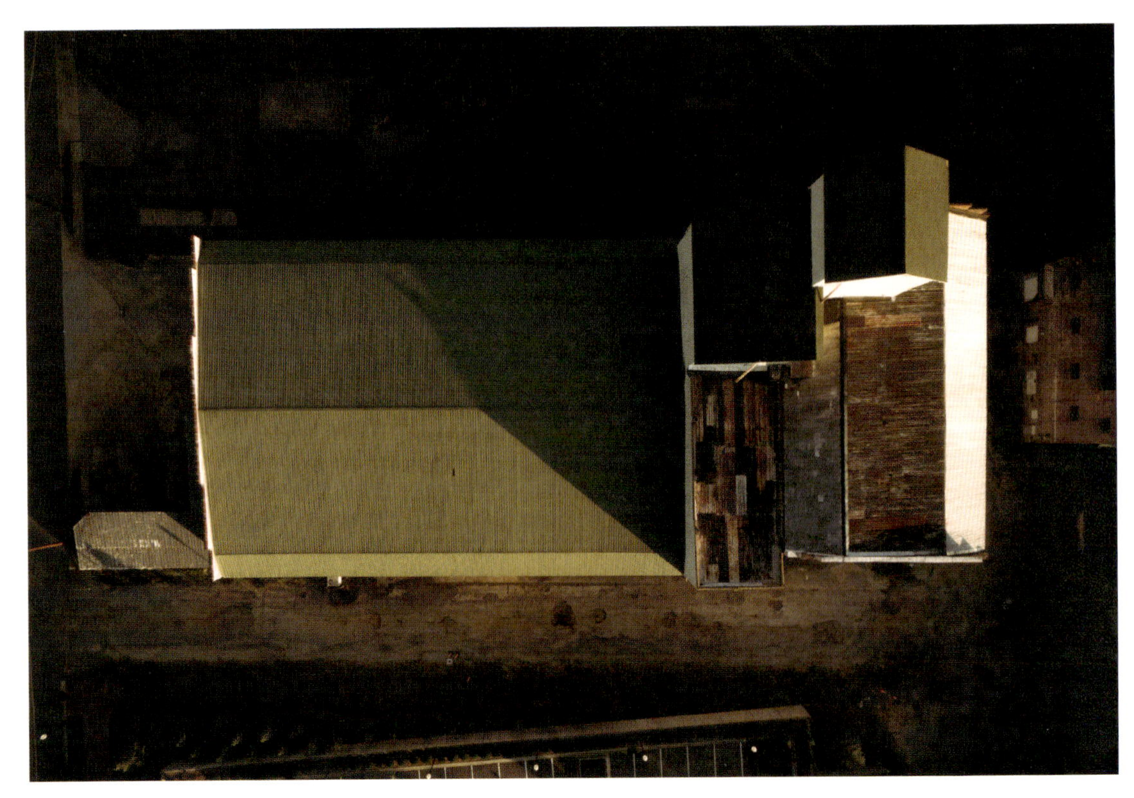

OLD SPARTAN GRAIN MILL

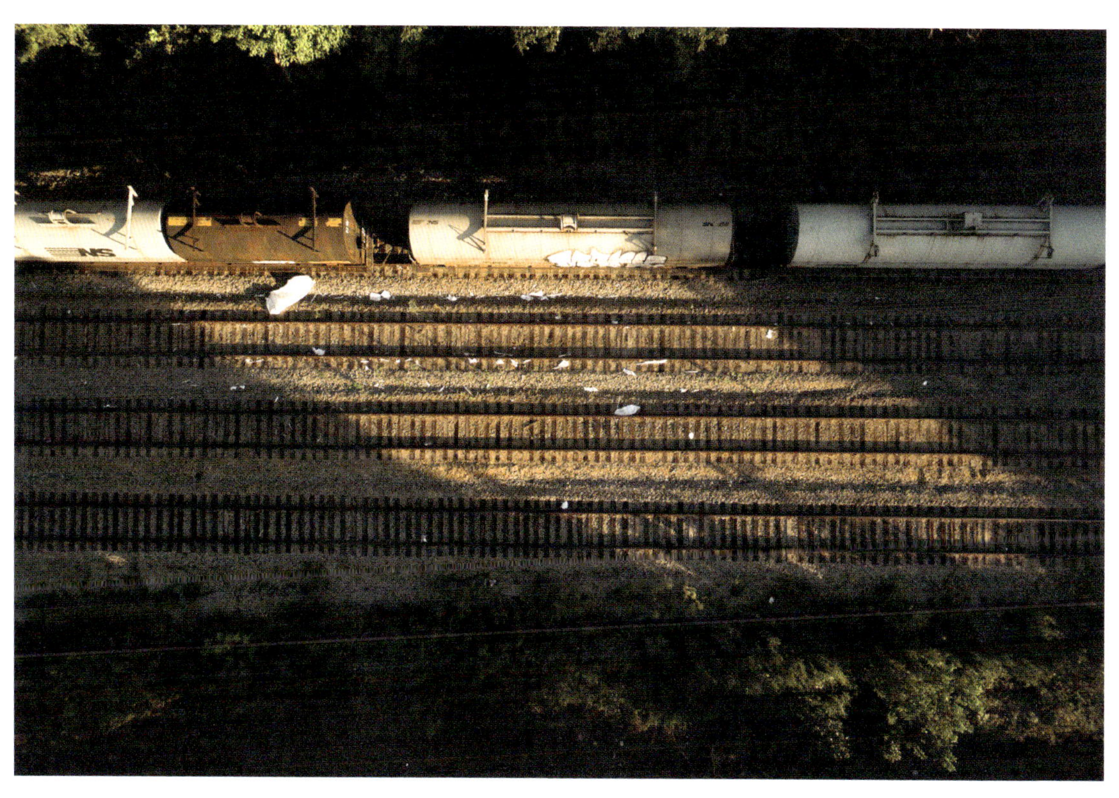

MEMORIAL DR TRACKS

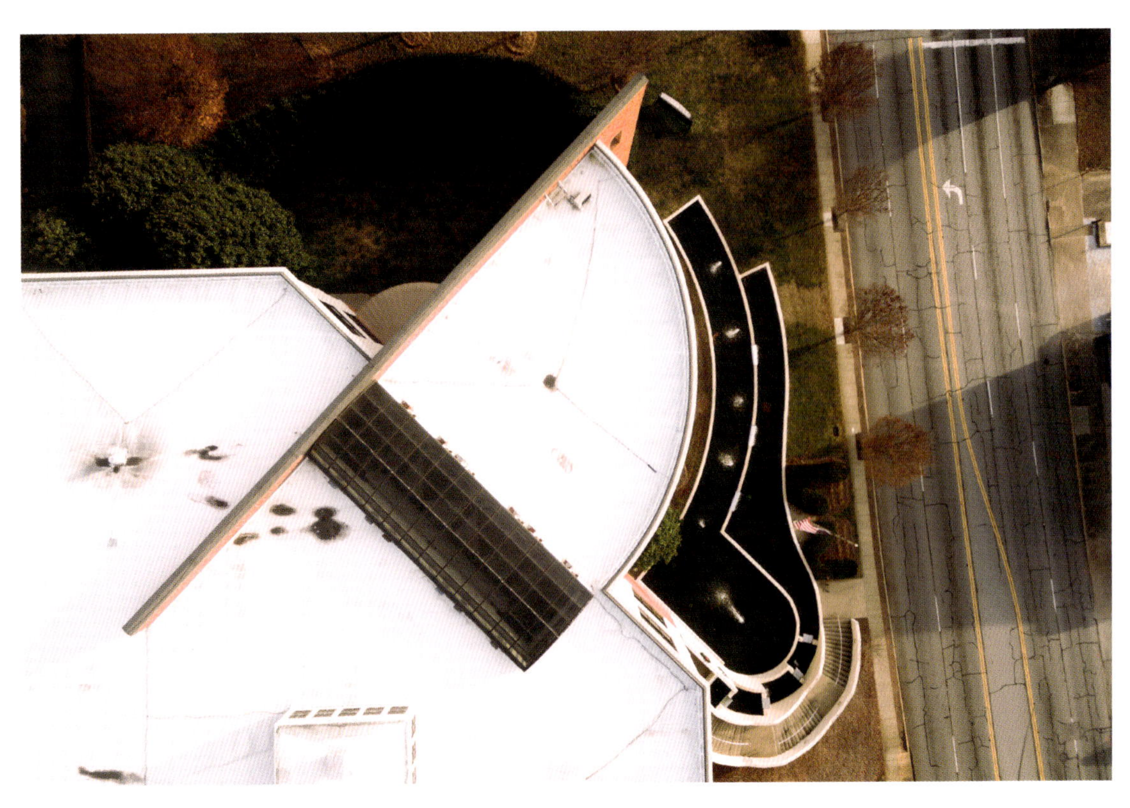

SPARTANBURG COUNTY PUBLIC LIBRARIES HEADQUARTERS

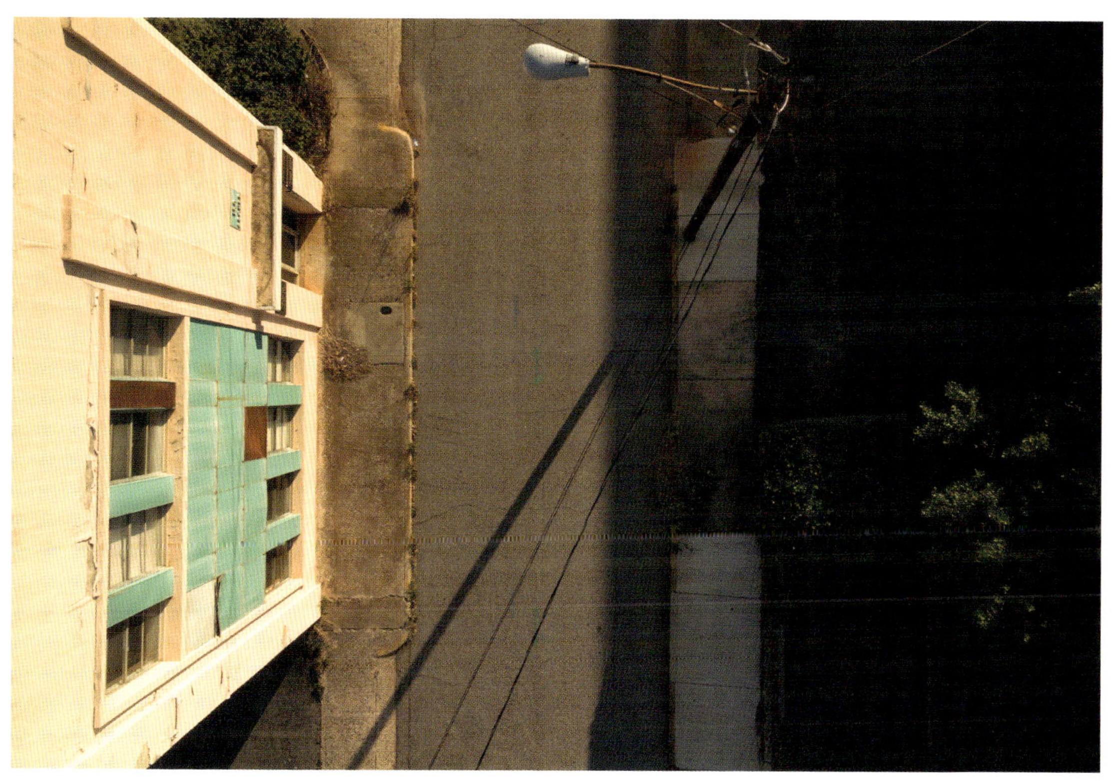

| ARCHER STREET

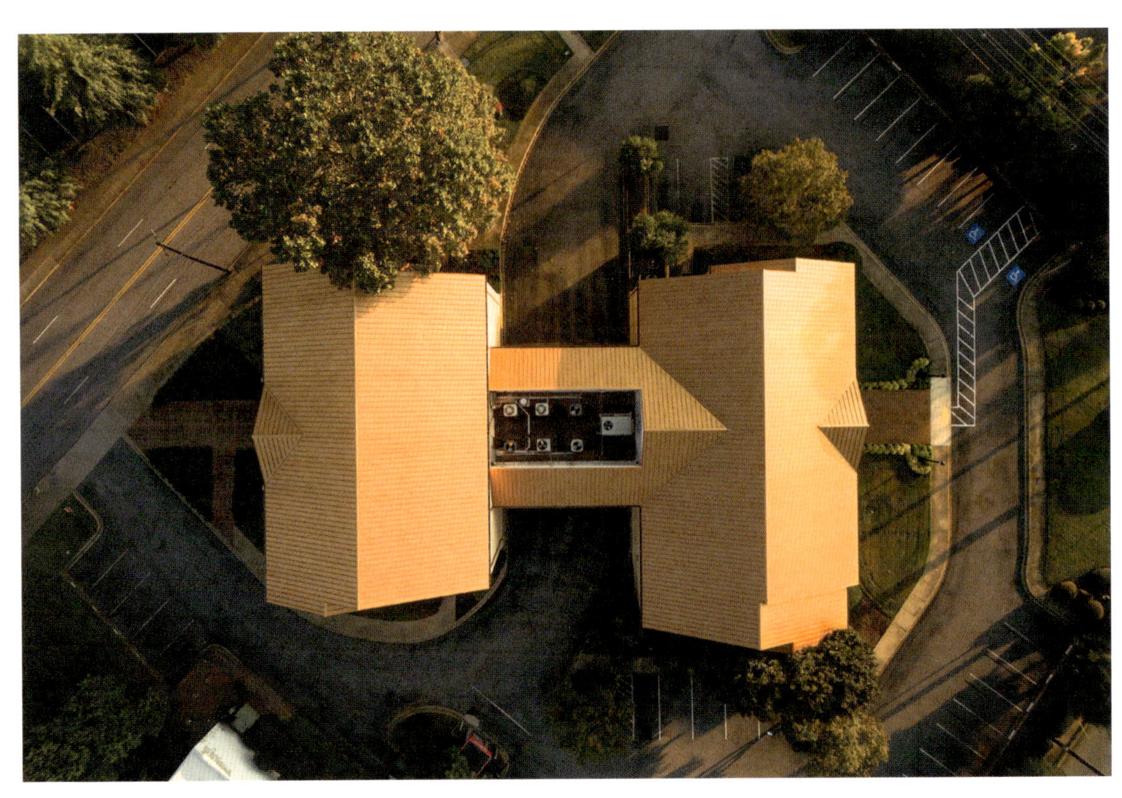

SYNOVUS BANK, W HENRY STREET |

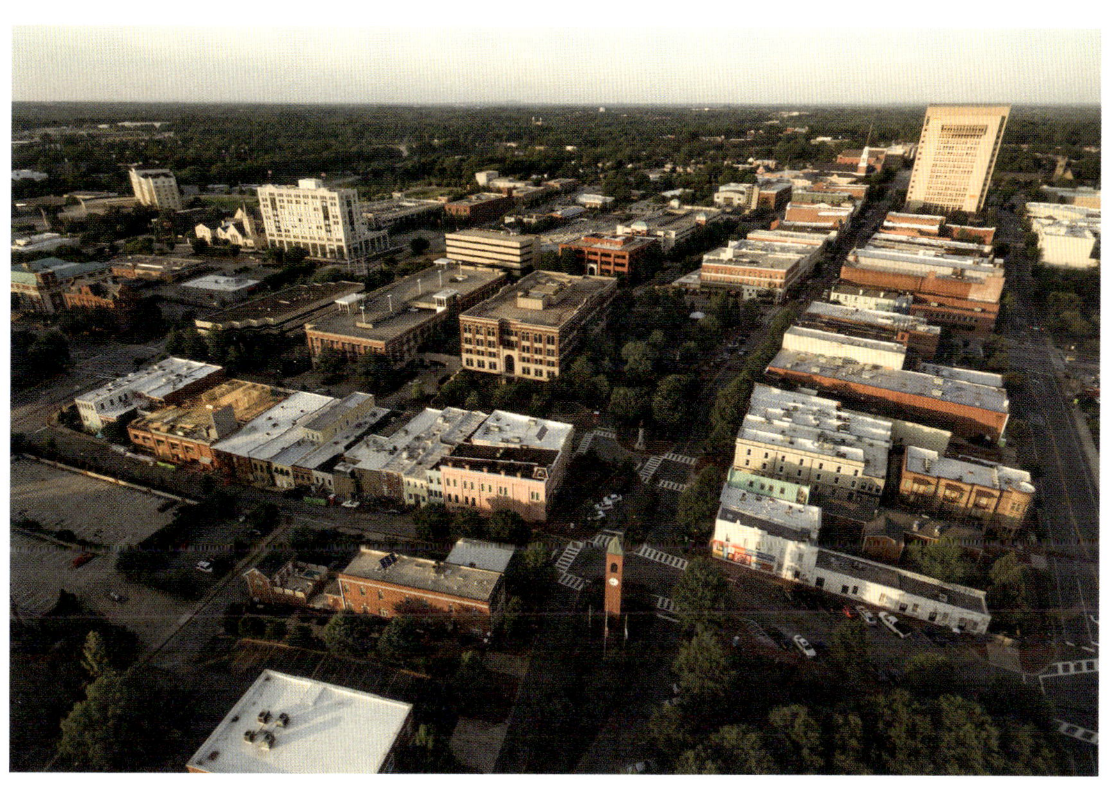

DOWNTOWN SPARTANBURG

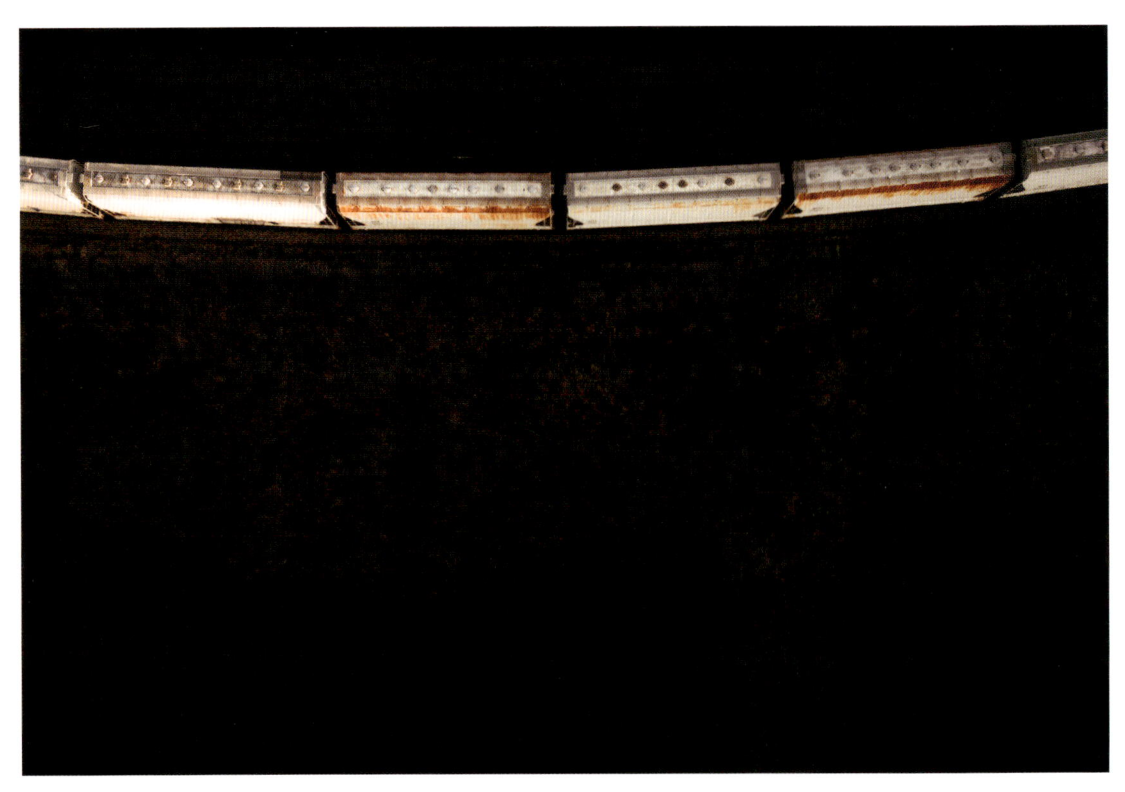

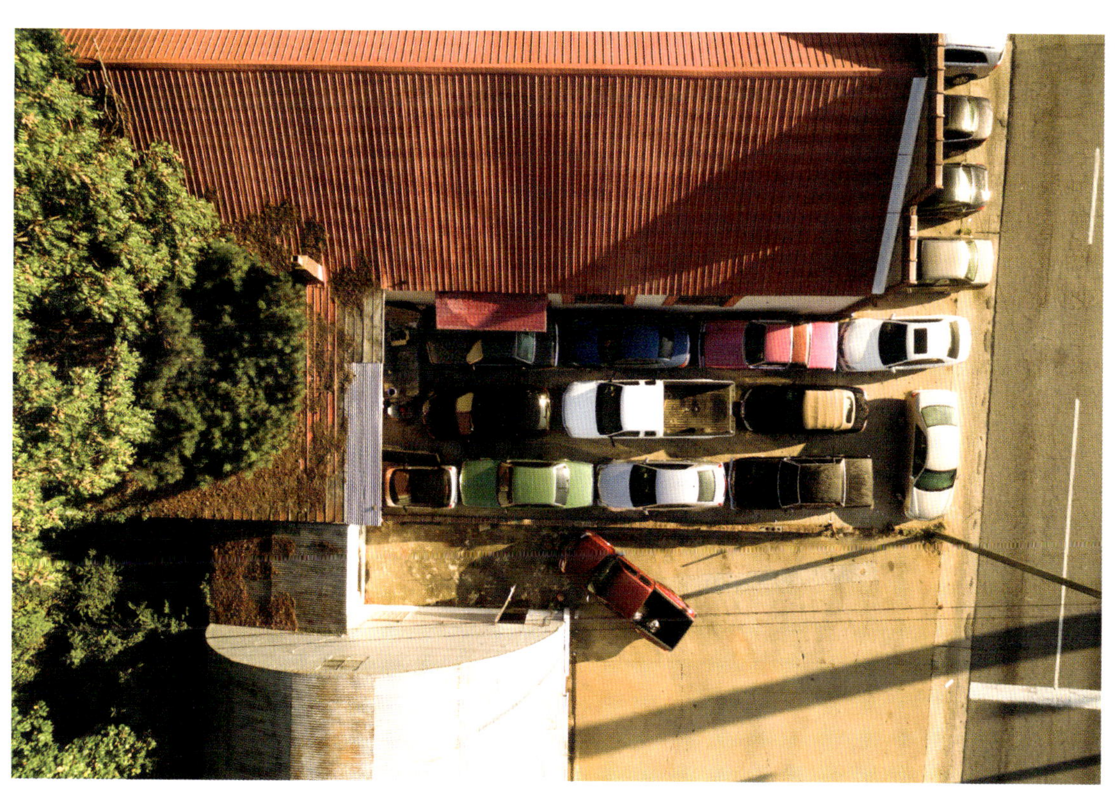

SPARTANBURG RADIATOR & MUFFLER

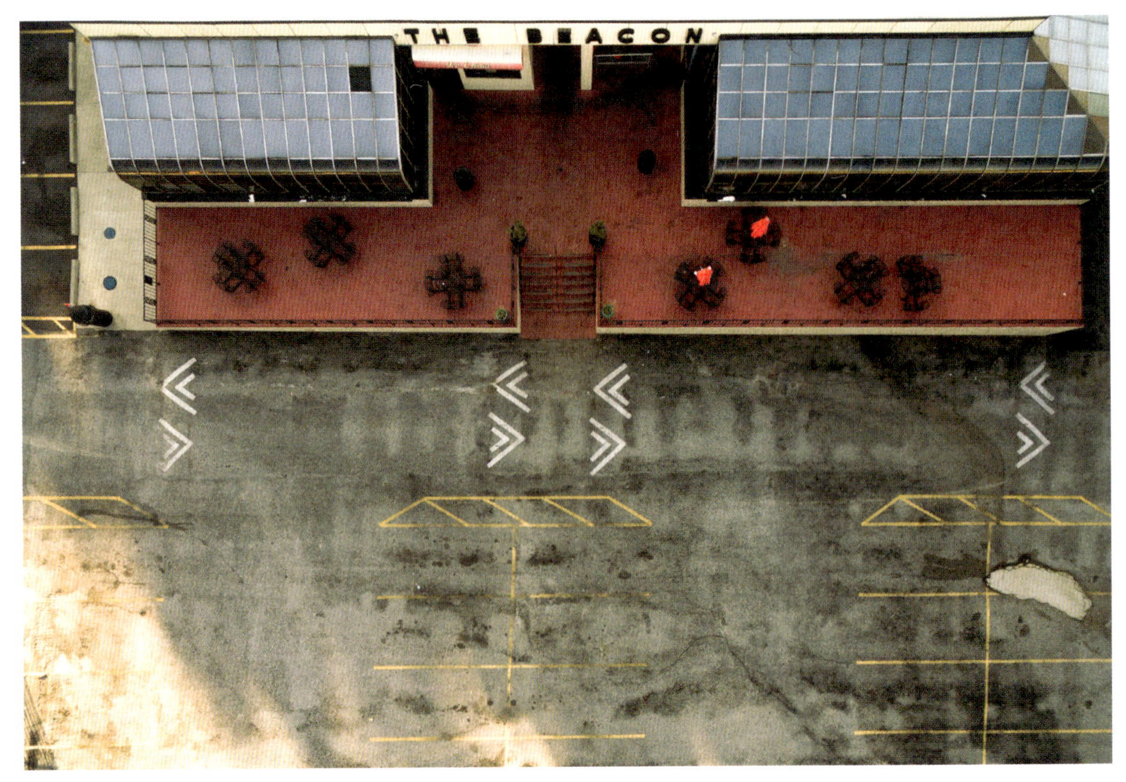

THE BEACON |

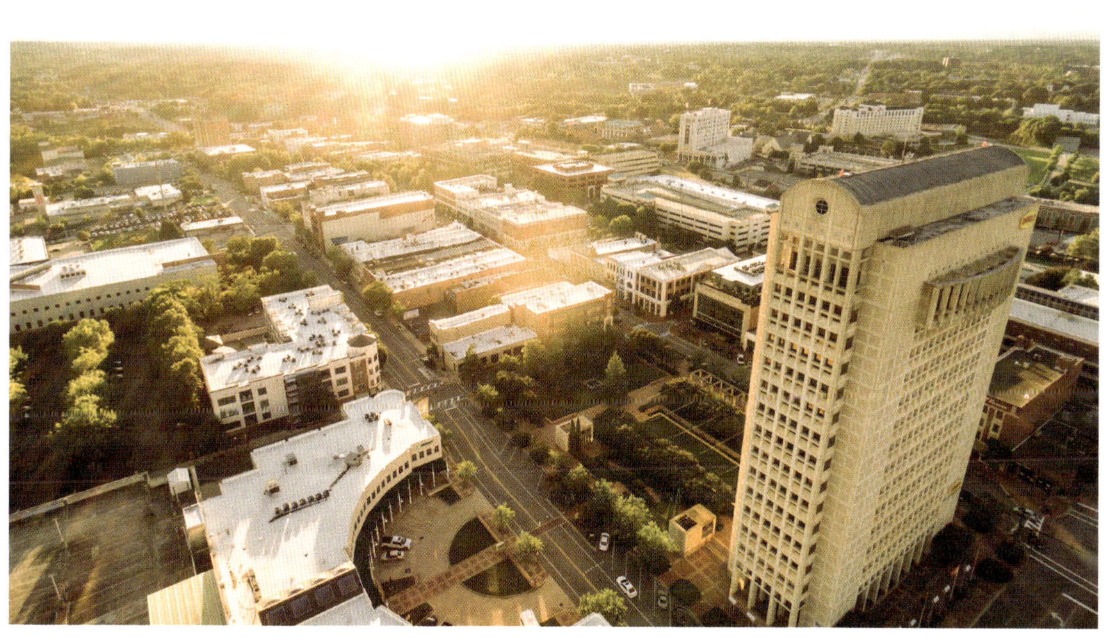

DOWNTOWN SPARTANBURG, SUNSET

WITH THANKS TO OUR GENEROUS SPONSORS

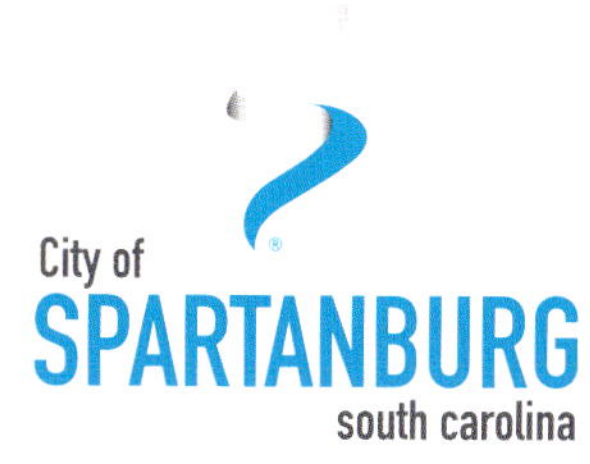

City of
SPARTANBURG
south carolina

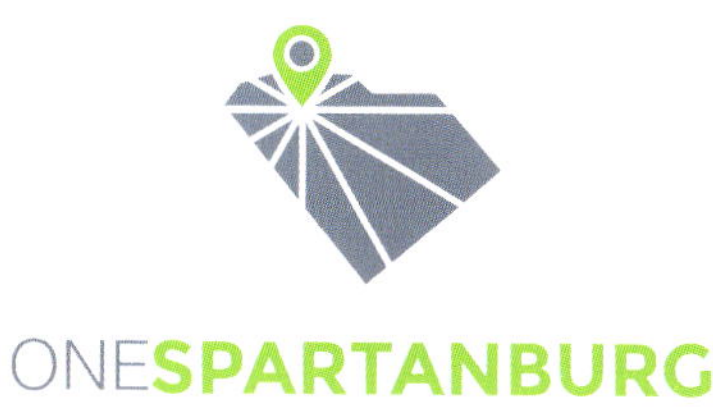

ONESPARTANBURG

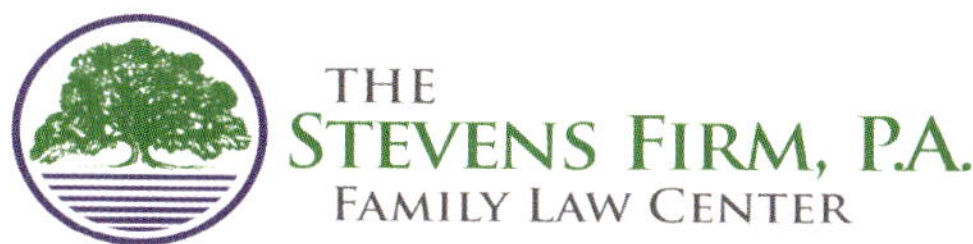

THE
Stevens Firm, P.A.
Family Law Center

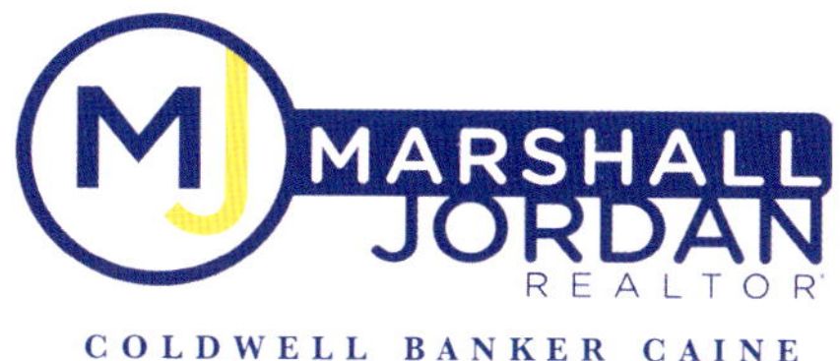

MJ MARSHALL JORDAN
REALTOR
COLDWELL BANKER CAINE

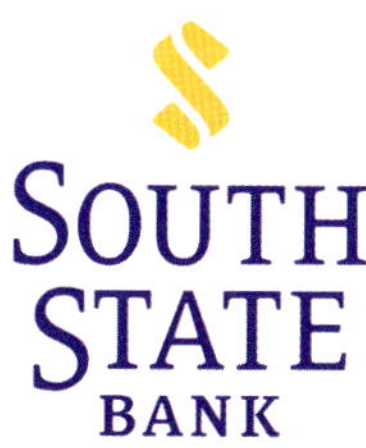

SOUTH STATE BANK

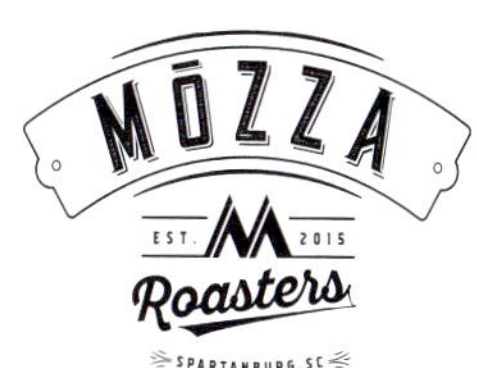

MŌZZA
EST. 2015
Roasters
SPARTANBURG, SC

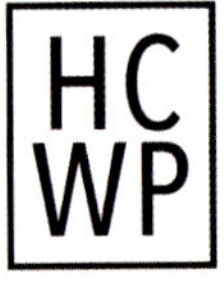 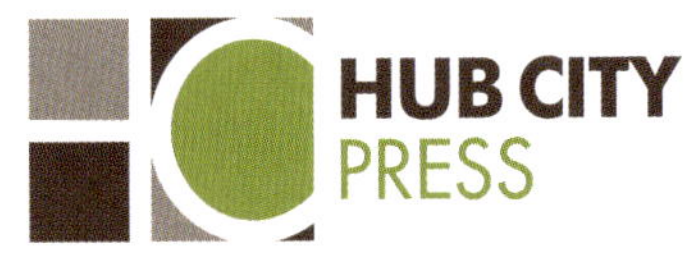

Hub City Writers Project is a new imprint of Hub City Press focused on highlighting Spartanburg voices. Founded in Spartanburg, South Carolina in 1995, Hub City Press has emerged as the South's premier independent literary press. Focused on finding and spotlighting new and extraordinary voices from the American South, the press has published over eighty high-caliber literary works, including novels, short stories, poetry, memoir, and books emphasizing the region's culture and history. Hub City is interested in books with a strong sense of place and is committed to introducing a diverse roster of lesser-heard Southern voices including: people of color, gender diversity, LGBTQIA, people with disabilities, as well as ethnic, cultural, and religious minorities.

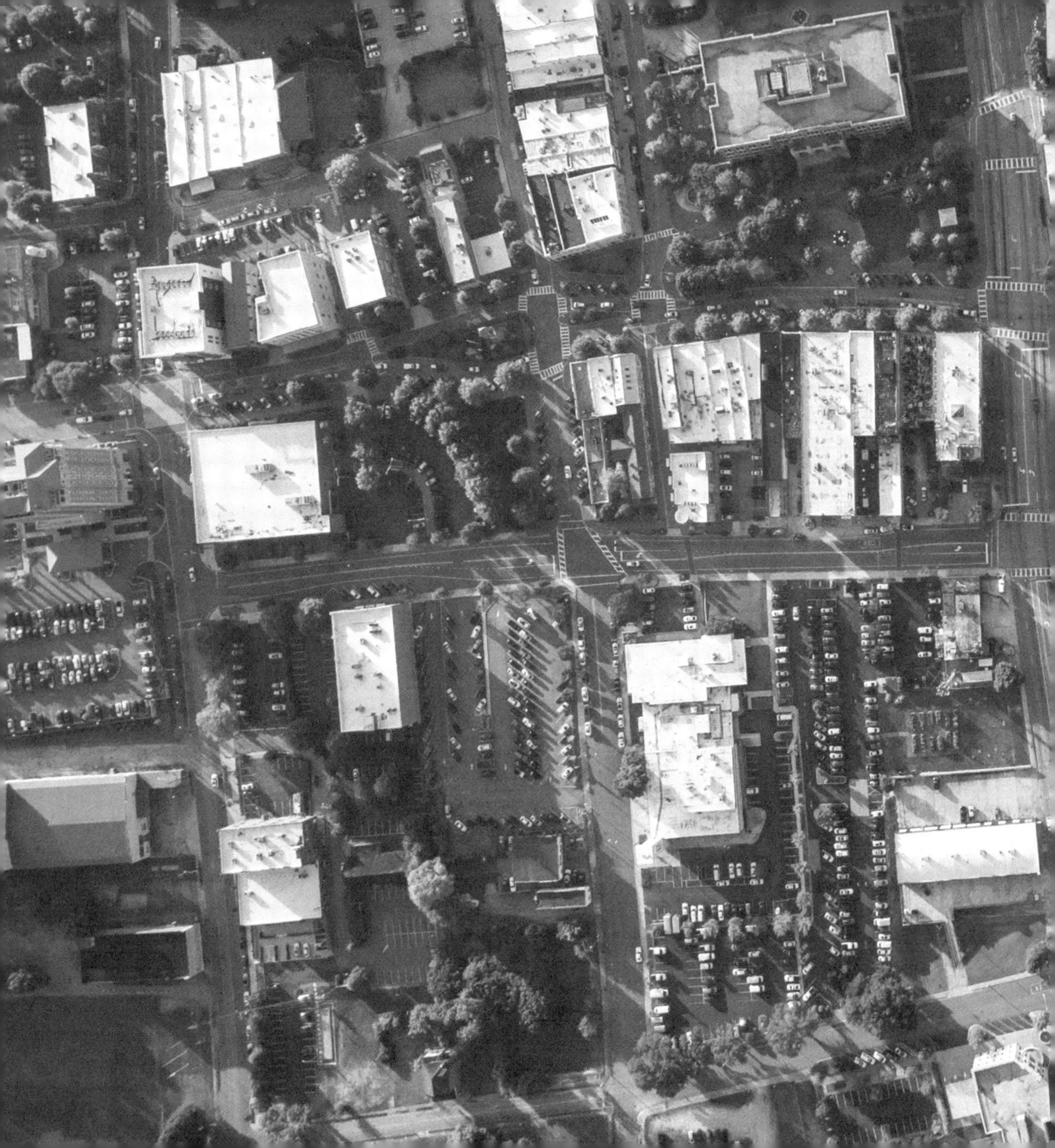